what seems to
be the problem?

what seems to be the problem?

A Restaurant Manager's Tale

Tobin Tullis

ABOOKS
Alive Book Publishing

What Seems to Be the Problem?
Copyright © 2014 by Tobin Tullis

Additional copies may be ordered from the publisher for educational, business, promotional or premium use. For information, contact ALIVE Book Publishing at: alivebookpublishing.com, or call (925) 837-7303.

Book Design by Eli Sedaghatinia

ISBN-13: 978-1-63132-002-6 Paperback
ISBN-10: 1631320025 Paperback

Library of Congress Control Number: 2014900185

Library of Congress Cataloging-in-Publication Data is available upon request.

First Edition

Published in the United States of America by ALIVE Book Publishing and ALIVE Publishing Group, imprints of Advanced Publishing LLC 3200 A Danville Blvd., Suite 204, Alamo, California 94507 alivebookpublishing.com

PRINTED IN THE UNITED STATES OF AMERICA

10 9 8 7 6 5 4 3 2 1

to

My dad because he never got the chance

for

My son to show him we can

because

My wife is the duct tape that
holds us all together

Contents

Introduction

"What seems to be the problem?" is the single term regurgitated table side by every manager from the greasy spoon to fine dining that sends chills up their spine. The green light to an unforeseen scenario that is certain to leave the manger scratching his head in wonder of the human race. I was that manager and this is where we dissect those scenarios to learn how not to be "that guy" while dining in or working at various watering holes.

Sometimes the only option is to cut bait and run, but how? To be a "foodie" is like being in the mafia. Every time you get out, they keep pulling you back in. I knew that if I didn't get out alive, nobody would, so here I document hope. Hope that there is life outside of food service. The key was to leave the better man for having learned so much in my 15 years there, but get out before it killed me.

From four distinctly different food venues, and a myriad of true stories that will drop jaws, we learn how to behave in the front of the house so we don't get talked about in the back.

"Most people get into the restaurant business for the wrong reasons"

Anthony Bourdain

PART I

An Unexpected Career

CHAPTER I

From the Ashes Rises a Career

I was life-stuck. Based on the way I had left home three years prior, nobody had any obligation to give me anything short of the middle finger. But sifting through the rubble and ashes of the wreckage I'd created, I would find compassionate people and an even more passionate career.

Just recently having had my still-beating heart removed from my chest by the "forever" woman with all the precision of an epileptic butcher, I had come home to the Bay Area from the greater Los Angeles basin. Alone and defeated, I had nothing more to go on than the support of the very people I had so adamantly said good-bye to "forever" as I started my quest for love and success in Southern California, expecting never to return.

I could crash back at my parents' pad, but ultimately that would only add another large log on the already raging fire of failure—and besides, why would I want to do that when I believed in my heart of hearts that Steve and his new girlfriend would love to have me stay indefinitely in their guest bedroom and pay him (never her) in scotch whisky for my room and board? Weeks turned into months, and looking back I don't even know how I managed to procure the funds for the obligatory bottle of Glen Fiddich on, or mostly around, the fifteenth of every month: a bottle, mind you, that I myself consumed half of with Steve and that was never used in any monetary sense to help ease the burden of the piling bills. My welcome mat was becoming more worn by the minute. Perhaps the warning signs were a little more clear than I was giving them credit for, like the vacuuming at 7:00 A.M. outside my door (and only my door). Wasn't there a whole house full of carpet? Or the fact that the very large dog that shared our space was suddenly given permission to sleep on my roll-out, where he was so adamantly forbidden from going before. The biggest indicator of just how receptive the lady of the house was to my squatting was the fact that I was never offered any sort of key that would allow me free access to where all my stuff was. And by all my stuff I am referring lovingly to my entire worldly possessions, which would fit snugly inside a medium-size duffel bag.

Didn't they understand that my heart was broken and all I needed was some time to get back on my feet, find a job, and secure some funds so I could head out to blaze my trail across this topsy-turvy blue marble we live on? Couldn't they possibly understand that I shouldn't accept a job at Starbucks or bagging groceries because I am far more valuable than that? I was just waiting for the right thing to come along, and while doing so inadvertently began my new life as a professional observer. I was actively watching everybody else come and go from their productive lives, while I watched reruns of *Family Feud* with a very large shedding dog, drinking scotch at 2:00 in the afternoon oblivious to my role in all this madness. Poor me, poor me, and pour me a drink.

My universe became apparent to me while sitting on the front porch one evening waiting patiently for my reluctant roommates to come home and open the door that I didn't have the key to. But not so very apparent, as later I would come home to find out that they'd gone on a weekend vacation without telling me... again, the indicators. In hour three of that mental standoff on the cold November porch I began to see my world for what it had become. Sad. Even my crazy friend Brendan had secured a decent job at a local country club as an assistant food and beverage manager (whatever that meant), and here I was still cursing the iron-hearted lady in L.A. who was probably at that very moment having sexual relations with my buddy she left me for. If nothing else, I knew she was indoors, the bottle of scotch they were drinking probably didn't double as rent, and they probably had a whole set of jingling keys between the two of them—monumentally more than I could say for myself.

It was time to swallow my ego pill and start over. I had no idea what the next fourteen minutes would hold for me, let alone the next fourteen years. All I knew was that it was morbidly liberating to be that low. I figured I would call Brendan tomorrow and see if I could wash dishes in his kitchen. I turned the key of my borrowed car and drove home.

Armed with a clear twenty-three-year-old head—mind you, the scotch was behind lock and key with the rest of my belongings—and the humility that comes in a package deal with being unemployed on a Monday, I drew a deep breath and called my best friend. Turns out that the country club in question was looking for a server and I should come down right away to speak to the general manger.

Pertinent is the fact that I had never worked in any sort of restaurant in any capacity ever, never seen an industrial kitchen, and couldn't tell a server from a busser if you dangled a lottery ticket in front of me—and at that point in time, there was nothing I wouldn't do for a lottery ticket (all I had was hope in those days). Truth be told, based on my recently depleted funds and throbbing heartache, I hadn't even set foot in anything higher-class than Fat Burger in the past six months, yet here I was thrusting the gas pedal down and blazing a trail toward my destiny in the restaurant biz.

Ignoring all the dramatic details of background checks, multiple interviews, and meetings with the financial giants in lofty positions who develop these sorts of oases, I somehow managed to finagle my first serving position at a level that still baffles me. It's good to have friends in hiring positions, and oh, the tapestry Brendan must have woven to get me in. I imagine that his hand was forced to create a work history for me that included years in every facet of the industry.

The club in question was a high-end private golf club with a course developed by none other than his holiness Jack Nicklaus. The fare and decor were Italian and the membership base was small, elite, and very wealthy. At this time in financial history, the greater Bay Area was knee-deep in its golden age, before the bubble burst; Silicon Valley was an erupting volcano spewing money all over a gaggle of thirty-somethings. Young budding familyites were buying an address in this gated community and barely having time to furnish their 24,000-square-foot house between rounds of golf and cocktails at the Tuscan clubhouse. This isn't just hyperbole; it was common knowledge that truly there were a few families living on air mattresses in bare-walled palaces because they were only interested in the address and had little time to furnish while feeding their other appetites for lush items.

In this rarefied world the executive chef reigned supreme, and the food and beverage, or F&B, director needed my friend more than ever while he himself schmoozed with all the new members in an effort to build a foundation of service, not to mention slake his own unquenchable thirst. Not only was I constantly amazed in my early days at the money and debauchery, but I was awestruck with Medieval feasting scene that wiped away all presumed boundaries between members and staff.

Internally a meaningful symbiotic relationship developed among the F&B director, his assistant (Brendan), the membership director, and later me. Together we would build and rule this gated empire and forge experiences that would have left Hunter S. Thompson scratching his head and saying *"Really?"*

Any specific experiences I had at this time were less significant than the fact that my head was completely peeled back, leaving my brain a fertile garden for the food business to plant its seeds in. Everything was enormous, shiny, and new: structural nuances of staffing and responsibilities, wine and what made for the perfect food pairing, more money invisibly circulating than could be counted in lifetimes by Wall Street, and the hours spent making sure all the cogs in the machine were running well or at least remained operational. The twelve-hour shift became the norm, and I only noticed the length of a day when Mondays rolled around and I had time to myself.

Most private clubs are closed on Mondays, allowing for necessary greens keeping and the staff incentive of free golf "on foot." This tradition further propelled my descent into this most exclusive of worlds, simply because my new management herd came equipped with a set of keys to this "sorry folks, were closed", Walley World for adults, allowing them to add the much-desired golf-cart accoutrement to our rounds. We would whisk past the lowly unfortunates who were forced to walk this 7,200-yard playground, and on any given day the wind and the heat made merely raising a golf club a daunting task, let alone trudging around with fifty pounds of equipment on your shoulder. Naturally, I found myself in what can only be described as a seventh heaven, far removed from the vixen who stole my soul in L.A. How could anyone with a pulse not get sucked into this world, hook, line, and sinker? A couple of weeks prior I had been sitting on a cold porch watching through a window as a dog got closer to my stuff than I could, and now I was a member (by default) at a private country club, and the only dues I had to pay was to work there. Brilliant!

My most integral relationship from this time would be forged with one very important person from our small four-person herd. I didn't know then how important she was to become in most facets of my life, both then and now, but reflect fondly on the sometimes harsh lessons that she provided when I was starting out. Juliann was the membership director at the time, but she started at the club in the humble underbelly of the Grille. This was a place where golfers stopped momentarily between holes 9 and 10 to stock up on provisions, and it was her entry level. But unable to contain the intelligence that she naturally possessed, Juliann was soon whisked into the position of event coordinator and then membership director. This was her title when I met her, but her title did her no justice. Making the most of any department would become her modus operandi. It was clear to every person either working or playing at this place of glory that Juliann ran the club and served more as assistant general manager to the "trouble with English" Indian fellow who officially held the reins. In short, she was a good person to have on your side and not a good person to cross.

I was fortunate that the small aforementioned herd of F&B director, his assistant Brendan, and Juliann chose me to be the fourth member of their band, saving me what surely would have been a humiliating display like the little cartoon dog running in circles around the bulldog asking, "Do ya wanna play now... do ya?" Together we forged on, learning, laughing, and sometimes falling down.

One of the first lessons taught me by the tireless Juliann came one night when I was a server. Every Friday night at the club was à la carte night: the membership came in droves dressed to the nines, having shed the kids to a sitter, and wanted a fine-dining three- to four-course meal of their selection. It was to the restaurant business what the major leagues are to the minors... "the show." Prior to every Friday night, the entire staff, all ten servers and four busboys, were gathered in a room to discuss menu alterations, wine service notes, and specials of the day, and we would be assigned sections on the floor where we would work that evening—a meeting known as the lineup. These were intensive tutorials that were an integral part of providing four-star services to the 150 guests arriving less than an hour hence.

On this day our assigned leader was absent and, being the chameleon of the club, Juliann became our substitute boss. Unfortunately in this instance she was being treated just like a substitute teacher in grammar school. The troops were not on their best behavior, and Juliann's lineup became a bit of a spit-wad-hurling, note-passing free-for-all. Tensions mounted. Being the epitome of cool was another of Juliann's strengths, and instead of hollering to get attention, chastising any one person for being disrespectful, or leaving the room in tears of defeat in the face of this pack of wild banshees, she simply sauntered over to the dry-erase floor plan that outlined the sections for the evening and grabbed the eraser. Everybody immediately settled into a jaw-dropping silence as she wiped the board clean of all names and boundaries and redrew a line down the exact middle of the dining room floor chart. She then wrote "Toby" on one side and "Tim" on the other, and turned to the now-attentive and very silent crowd of well-dressed servers and bussers. She said calmly, "If you don't see your name here on this chart, go home," and left the room. Guess what? She meant it.

In a much smaller lineup that followed with just Juliann, me, and Tim, she reassured us that we could do this together, and with teamwork it would all work out. She didn't sugarcoat how difficult the night was going to be. She didn't try to gloss over the 110 reservations on the books for the evening, or the fifteen table sections Tim and I were each responsible for. She just gave us a line that I still use today in management: "No matter what, there are still only sixty seconds in a minute and sixty minutes in an hour, and that time will pass at the same rate as it did yesterday"—meaning that really, it will all be over sooner than you think. Needless to say, I was introduced to the phenomenon of "the weeds" that evening. (*Sidenote: The "weeds" are the mental state that every server has been to where the demands of the customers far outnumber the deliveries being made and the list just keeps getting longer resulting in one of two outcomes: 1. Asking for help and thereby admitting your not superhuman—surprisingly difficult for most servers—or, 2. Monumental , and often animated public meltdown.)* Even so, no food got sent back, no members got up and left, and Juliann and I formed a bond based on respect for each other that is still the foundation of our friendship today. She also taught me without words the most profound lesson I have ever learned, and that is that nobody is indispensable. Just ask the eight servers and four bussers who went home for the evening.

In retrospect the countless hours I was putting in at the club could be perceived as demonstrating an incredible work ethic, but my dirty little secret was that I couldn't wait to get there. In the spare moments before and after my shift, the executive chef was verbally walking me through the facets of the "back of the house," the bartender was grooming me as his go-to barback, the sommelier would look for me to taste the latest wine to come in, the hostesses were showing me how to put together an operational floor plan for every occasion, the membership director was telling me details of members' likes and dislikes so that I got their dining experience right every time, and the F&B director was teaching me scheduling, Profit &Loss projection models and, most important, how to balance a professional demeanor on the outside even if my insides were churning: "Never let them see you sweat."

I was a sponge that could never be saturated. I wanted it all... and damned if I didn't get it. I became head server one year after starting, dining room manger a year after that, and food and beverage director a year later. I was on the fast track through management. Not bad considering that three years prior I had held the dubious moniker of "one table Mabel," thanks to my inability to cut short tableside conversation in order to take care of more than one table on a busy night. However, with this newfound passion came the responsibility of handling people's complaints and being subjected daily to the one human attribute that still baffles me to this day.

Twelve-step programs call the phenomenon of the beginning days of any experience "little pink clouds," and any veteran of rebuilding will quickly tell you to make sure that your little pink clouds have "little pink parachutes," because the clouds will disappear and leave you in a free-fall. I soon realized that on the playing field of food service I must have a game face and kill the paying customers with kindness and acceptance; but behind the scenes and in the comfort of my own world, I needed to come up with some way to blow off steam. I needed a way to tell the people who acted out in bizarre ways that their behavior was catapulting them to the status of potential assholes, and customers or not, they were all wrong. I wanted to produce a manual of sorts, one that would not only allow restaurantgoers to learn things they may not have previously known about dining out, but at the same time make direct examples of the jerkoffs who over the years have inspired me to lay out the unwritten rules to dining out, all the while keeping them laughing and yelling over their shoulder at their counterpart in the other room, "Honey, can you believe what this guy did at a restaurant?" Of course she can, Gomer. That guy is you! This is that manual. The second part of this book deals with how I got out! My exit strategy may not work for everybody, but then let my story reflect the true existence of greener pastures.

Personal Credentials

What exactly gives me the right to believe that I have enough life experience in any capacity to even entertain the idea of regurgitating past events and philosophies over the unsuspecting general public? Just exactly what greasy spoon did I come from, and do I really believe that whatever has happened in my storied past makes for entertaining reading? Well, yes, in fact, I do.

Any person who has tasted the blood of anger tableside; or sweated so profusely that the bartender thought it best to stop trying to stanch the salty brow fall and make a featured cocktail out of it; or unwillingly cried the tears of not only frustration from being unable to extricate oneself from "the weeds," but those tears of mourning a lost patron or of happiness from a properly paid compliment or tip, is in fact himself a fully accredited expert on the subject. In my case, I was blessed early on with credentials from four very different venues that cover the spectrum of anything that is possible in the food service industry. Out of respect for the venues themselves and their possible reluctance to have my personal opinions aired publicly, I will not divulge their names, but suffice it to say that in hindsight at least, I hold each one in the highest regard in the arenas of professionalism, teaching human behavior, and opportunities for radical personal growth.

The Private Golf Club

The first prestigious battleground was the aforementioned country club, a Tuscan-style private golf club that catered to the whimsy of young money. It was a real estate development put on the planet for the sheer purpose of associating a physical address with the résumés of some very top executives and their families, a playground of debauchery that for me was an appetizer to the craziness of F&B. The scenes that played out on those grounds will forever be etched in my memory for the sheer reason that they were the first. You never forget your first, even if she was some grossly obese person with a lazy eye and you just happened to have a couple extra dollars in your pocket and a hollow leg full of Southern Comfort .

Needless to say, the club became the first act of my budding and seemingly endless F&B career. It was here that I had my proverbial cherry popped and witnessed things that would both excite and frighten me to the depths and beyond of my previous understanding of my own personal thresholds. Because this country club was private and was either offered to or available to only a very elite few, the bonds formed between staffers like myself and the paying clientele had very undefined lines, and our lives constantly bled into one another. One minute I was honing my craft by creating recreation programs for the children of the young socialites, and the next I was going over to their parents' houses after the children had been tucked into bed for the night and drinking until dawn with the very people who were providing my modest salary to serve as a prim and proper example for their brood. The irony was never wasted on me, to say the least. I would describe a typical day working and breathing well within the gated community that consumed me, but the days were never typical.

Summer was an amazingly busy time at the club. The Men's Invitational tournament, which took me to the outer edge of sanity and to my breaking point by requiring four sixteen-hour days of hard work in a row, was a mere footnote to the season. Summer was also the time for the growing-in-popularity Kids Camp that Juliann and I developed. It being summer, the little ones living in the community lacked the structure and tutelage provided by the school year and in turn, the parents were lacking their minds and common sense. It became clear to me on more than one occasion, though certainly not across the board, that some of these young socialites were ill prepared for the responsibilities that come with parenthood and probably only procreated by mistake on some tequila-fueled night of passion in Cabo San Lucas. The children in question were constantly being handed from one care provider to the next by the very people responsible for their existence. The warm summer nights and open-ended schedules during the day that allowed the kids with free time to flap endlessly in the breeze provided the inspiration for creating the summer program.

For one week in August the children (approximately fifteen to twenty of them, ages five to twelve) were dropped off at the tennis and swim center at 7:00 A.M. and retrieved at 4:00 P.M. by the parents who were just wrapping up their own afternoons of golf and tennis. Caregiver by day and friend by night, I couldn't wait until the little tykes were in bed for the evening so I could go over to one of their mansions and drink my way through the wine cellar. In short: "Why, yes, I will help round out your children's experience here and try my very best to make them advanced little humans through the example that I set" was promptly followed by "Yes, I believe I will have another glass of the 1968 Châteauneuf du Pape, and please pass the Brie." I was a whore for the experience. Those days at the camp were exhausting, and consisted of a different outdoor activity daily; two prepared and provided meals; sports classes pertinent to the club life such as golf clinic, tennis clinic, and so on; daily swim; and arts and crafts, all planned and executed for five days straight.

On one particular day in question, the memory of which so easily whisks me back to that time of my life, I was invited to attend (not work) a huge charity ball in the evening at the soccer field inside the gates. As frivolous as these people may have seemed to be during the day, they were philanthropic, and their influence drew thousands of people and dollars annually to the charity ball and a select few very worthy nonprofits in our community. In the past I had provided services at the ball such as bartending, valet service, or ushering, but this year I had to rent a tux as I was a guest—which in hindsight was symbolic of my time inside the gates. I rented my life, never really owned it like everybody else. The only snafu was that the ball this year was on the same day as Kids Camp. Not an impossible endeavor, but challenging to say the least. The kids were tended to properly and got the freshest of us, then retrieved at the four o'clock hour and shuttled to the sitters while I retreated to my one-bedroom apartment five miles away to unsheathe and don my rented Selix, sneering at the pathetic environment I called "home," which I could barely afford.

Then "To the bat cave!" and back to club and the ball. Beer gave way to wine and cocktails as minutes gave way to hours, and fuzzy are the details that found me swimming (in my underwear) at a nearby member's house at four in the morning. Fuzzier still are the details that led to my hurried walk of shame down the main street of the enclave at sunrise, hoping beyond all hope that no employees or members would be out at 6:00 A.M. on a Saturday morning as I tried to make it back to my car on the other side of the compound, barefoot, holding damp dress shoes and half jogging. It was imperative that I be quick in order not to get caught, but more important, I needed to get back ASAP in order to work the wedding being held that day at the club, as I hoped beyond all hope that nobody in my inner circle would be any wiser about my fantastic double life. Funny thing is, days like those never seemed abnormal at the time; I only saw them as ludicrous later in life, and even now I remember them fondly with a smile.

San Francisco Bar and Grill

If cutting my teeth in fine dining was the rose garden out in front of the amusement park, there was no doubt that my time at this second establishment was the roller coaster inside.

Shortly after I left the increasingly inbred grounds of the golf club in pursuit of a higher education, a dear friend and one-time co-manager at the golf club departed as well and opened a seventy-five-seat bar and grill in the heart of the financial district in downtown San Francisco. A phone call and a meeting led to him asking me to be a sweat equity partner (build a client base and reap the benefits). These sacred walls would become the bard to many a tale of profit and debauchery. This was a classic San Francisco eatery and watering hole, with its thirty-seat oak bar stretched in front of four huge arched windows providing a perfect front-row view of the commerce that is day-to-day life in the financial district on Sacramento Street. The address said "Go earn your money, ants," but the neon signs said "But you might as well stop for a quickie before you do." And believe you me, they stopped at all hours of the morning and night. After I had successfully built a reliable clientele, the routine of "one for me and one for you" became the everyday norm, and by the end of four years I had drunk and snorted my way out of the S.F. food and beverage business forever, holding on to the last shreds of health and sanity that remained.

But in those four years I tightrope-walked with, once again, my brain completely peeled back and in awe of my immediate surroundings. If I was going to work in the city, I realized, I needed to immerse myself in the urban sprawl. I adopted a Jane Goodall kind of mentality: if I was going to serve these people hamburgers and Martinis properly, then I must live among them as a native. Needless to say, this would not be the first, nor the last episode in my life that would be chalked up as "the best time I would never do again."

Living in Oakland and working in San Francisco allowed me the benefit of having a chauffeur service. Sure, a lot of people called it Bay Area Rapid Transit (BART) and even considered it to be set up for them as well, but make no mistake about it, BART was mine and created for "my" needs, though I was happy to let them use it. This freed up any time spent on the job worrying about the precarious balance between social drinking and safe driving. I had discovered that in order not to drink and drive, all you had to do was quit driving. Turns out I had been thinking about it all wrong for so long.

The cast of characters for my new production was overwhelmingly colorful: bike messengers who stayed gainfully employed in the e-mail era merely by adding cocaine to their list of services for delivery; the morning drinkers who ate mints religiously thinking that peppermint was a fix all for alcoholism on their way back to the office; and my favorite, the young gunner twenty-somethings recently released from their college campus armed with a degree, a trust fund, and the vigor to single-handedly turn the financial world upside down. These guys traveled in herds and would roll in about 3:00 every afternoon, shortly after the market closed. The most remarkable attribute of this clan of future Alcoholics Anonymous patrons was that they would never sit down. Literally, they would stand at the bar and drink Ketel One and sodas while waiting for the bike messenger to deliver their valuable powdered parcels, at which point they'd loosen their ties and spend the next three hours high-fiving each other over past sorority triumphs. They quickly became dubbed the "high-fiving white guys," and they were good for business because they all had shiny new expense accounts and didn't wear down our bar stools.

The parameters of my professional guidelines were redefined in a single act of desperation on our first St. Patrick's Day, in an act that would become as much a part of the institution as the beer taps and liar's dice cups. We were six deep all day at the bar, a never-ending mob of people waving money and shouting orders. My friend the owner and I were the only bartenders and rarely had a chance to look up, let alone stop and breathe, save for the occasional Bacardi 151 shot that we quickly downed while on the run to the next thirsty patron.

Around hour five of this melee I needed a ten-minute break, for the simple purpose of sitting down to wring out my socks, but the break was not justified and could not be fitted into this barrage of thirsty people wearing tall green hats and free shiny beads provided by Guinness. So my scheming mind came up with what would later be dubbed "Coyote REAL Ugly." I slipped into the kitchen and hiked up my shin-length apron to take off my pants (thank God I was wearing tighty whities that day, as this became a standard uniform for every St. Patrick's Day to follow).

On my way back to the bar I filled my apron pocket with the green beads and set the stereo to some very loud hip-hop to cut through the crowd noise and suggest audibly to the unsuspecting afternoon drinkers that something might be about to happen. (*Sidenote: I have always loved the wave reaction that happens when you alter the audio environment in a busy place. You jack the music up and watch the look of anticipation and confusion wash across the faces of the public, their eyes darting this way and that trying to be the first person to see "it" coming, whatever "it" is going to be.*) I then jumped up on the bar top and began to do a stomach-churning, pole worthy dance while helicoptering beads above my head and encouraging young female executives to "show us your tits." The crowd amped itself into a frenzy and people began waving dollar bills in my direction, but most important, they collectively forgot how important it was to order that next drink, allowing me the much-deserved break that I needed.

Around minute twelve I looked back at my friend behind the bar and saw that he was getting the much-deserved break he needed as well, as commerce had stalled for the moment. With my apron now long removed from my waist and my tighties hiked up my ass crack, I revealed the pièce de résistance when I removed my shirt and my far-too-hairy-for-public-display Buddha belly came rolling out above the unsuspecting crowd. Twenty-five minutes later and with BVDs stuffed full of ones, I exclaimed in my best Tom Cruise fashion, "Bar's Open!" and on into the night we trudged, armed with the knowledge that I just might have created something that would have to be repeated on an annual basis.

Little did I know in future years that this seemingly isolated event would have me shopping at Victoria's Secret in the first weeks of March, picking out matching panties and socks that would really make the routine pop, or that an 8½ x 11 glossy of me (fully clothed) splayed on a bear-skin rug would be adorning the menu box out front reminding people weeks in advance to come see Toby and his St. Paddy's Day "Coyote REAL Ugly." I came to realize that these are the things that one learns about oneself in the arena of food and beverage service that one would never be privy to while manning a cubicle somewhere waiting for five o'clock to arrive. At the same time, these are the sorts of things you discover about yourself that you would never brag about to your mother or bring up at Thanksgiving dinner. Such a fun slippery slope, but I had to get out of San Francisco before I hurt somebody—namely, myself.

Hiatus Hiccup

Freshly armed with the belief that this sort of occupation was far too entertaining and dangerous to be considered a "real job," and filled with the knowledge that F&B is a tough row to hoe for the long haul, I was actively pursuing my degree in higher learning all the while I was working at the bar and grill in San Francisco. I'd be damned if I wasn't going to have a job that the masses could be proud of hearing about and discussing around the family dinner table. If nothing else, I would be in possession of a career that they could all wrap their collective minds around, as Lord knows they couldn't quite understand Coyote REAL Ugly.

This most certainly would have to take the form of cubicle work so that the family and close friends could read the comic strip *Dilbert* to find out how my life was going and fill in the missing pieces of how regular folk live. Just think of the time I would save not having to give the verbal updates myself when Scott Adams was drawing them so eloquently on a daily basis. So I did. I earned a BS in business management and promptly scoped out the lucky three half-walls that would come to stifle my extroverted personality in the name of the American dream. (*Sidenote: the acronym "BS" is not wasted on me when talking about my degree.*) These vast fields of office wheat in their infinite silence and hypnotic un-inspiration were where I learned that I had not just been bitten by the restaurant bug, but the wound had become disgustingly infected like a canker sore you can't stop poking with your tongue. Not long into my two-year adventure as a cubicle rat, I became acutely aware of the sound of the ticking clock.

This is not a metaphor. From two rooms away for eight hours a day, I was tormented by the fact that I could, plain as day, make out the tick... *eternity*... tock of the wall-mounted Seiko in the break room. I was not even considering a return to the restaurant floor of a food establishment at the time; all I could truly wrap my mind around was that this was no way to live for a person who had become so used to the controlled chaos of a busy dining room or shopping for panties in March. I began to imagine what would happen if I leaped up on my desk one day and did Coyote REAL Ugly for the other lifeless minions in the office. My hypothesis was that it would not go well, so I left that briefcase world behind and went looking for my long-lost bear-skin rug and my Victoria's Secret charge card.

The Steak House

Let it be known that I did not do the "right thing" and line something up before quitting the cubicle maze that had held me captive for far too long. The necessity of removing myself from the grips of corporate America and the little Napoleon named Hector who was my direct supervisor in the cubicle life took precedence over any appropriate resignation tactics that I firmly believed in. I simply walked away from both.

Because of the ill-advised manner in which I "took this job and shoved it," I was magically whisked back to a mini version of where I started this whole down-and-out debacle, and by the time I became gainfully employed again I would have washed dishes. I returned to my hometown that I had so successfully run away from time and again and started cold-calling restaurants in a shirt and tie. The dress code will be addressed shortly, but I am convinced that this was the deciding factor in my quest. Ties can be far more valuable than even the information on your résumé.

Suffice it to say that I did not choose the steak house, the steak house chose me. I merely walked in the door and asked if the manager was available. All I knew was that to make a good run at this restaurant life, I needed to do it in a career-driven way. I was going to remove myself from the tipped employee realm once and for all, and work as a manager while striving to become a general manager, then one day perhaps an owner. I became convinced that this was the only path to success in the business, but just like the best-laid plan, it did not work out that way... at first. The only position I could secure was that of a server, as there were no openings at the steak house for a manager. This became the "Let me think about it... okay" moment that would change everything. I started my five-day training process as a server, and on day five was pulled aside by the GM and asked if I would still like to be a manager. This was based solely on the fact that one of the other managers was leaving, not so much on my stellar five-day performance or storied past; but my father could still be heard to say, "What took them so long?"

The key became to work for the right person who could mold my potential GM status in the shortest amount of time. Mentally I was giving the process five years as a floor manager. I was blessed with that opportunity at the steak house and under the tutelage of Kevin the GM.

Let's go to the tale of the tape. The restaurant was two miles from my house. The venue was fine-dining and privately owned, and I was to be one of three managers on the floor (not counting the sommelier, who had key-carrying authority). Everything seemed primed and ready for launch. Here I was made to wear a suit jacket nightly, as the phenomenon of management in a coat might ease the atrocity of your steak being undercooked more adequately than the slack-jaw in merely a tie. In addition to the suit jacket I became responsible for the nightly financial reporting of the activity in the building, which was a gigantic leap in training to be a GM. (*Sidenote: to enter the fast track to upper management, suggest/demand that you have access to the financial books. This will skyrocket any individual to not only cold, hard knowledge of the business, but also to the "trust" of your superiors, when done properly.*)

However, the training and knowledge aside, the most invaluable gift I would receive from this stage of my career was the perspective it provided on the "dining out" experience as a whole. Not unlike my other foodie positions in the past, my mind was again being peeled back in an unquenchable thirst for knowledge, but not in the fashion that I had grown accustomed to. Having to handle and accept responsibility for any situation that veered away from perfect in the minds of the individuals who were spending their carefully cultivated coin in our establishment became exhausting, yes, but also fascinating. Here I was not a footsoldier like at the golf club, and the owner was not my good friend like in San Francisco, where I could tell an unruly patron, "Get the fuck out." I was a slave to the customer service side, responsible for getting them to come back.

The situation constantly called for my tableside smile, suggesting and solidifying the old adage "The customer is always right," and I had recourse to the oh-so-valuable phrase "What seems to be the problem?" on a nightly basis. However, on the inside I was churning. Not only were the customers *not* always right, they were pretty much constantly wrong. Not always dramatically (though oftentimes yes), not always to the point of sweeping the contents from the table with one foul motion of the arm in disgust (though I would have liked to do that very thing more than once), and not always in the "don't let them see you grind your teeth down to nubs behind pursed lips" way (though secretly I was doing just that), but all I really wanted in those days was the ability to yell at these miscreants, "Get the fuck out!" as I had been able to do in the past.

What was really happening was that I was unsuspectingly creating the fodder for this tutorial that I am scribing right now. The steak house experience was gelling nicely with my previous F&B experiences, and lessons were being cultivated not only in dining etiquette but in human nature and how to live in coexistence with all the others that walk on two legs around us, if only in the places we go to dine. A manual, if you will, on showing the masses what I have learned through sheer observation and the personal quest not to end up in front of a judge being sentenced to anger management classes.

Over time, the passion became so overwhelming that I just had to release my pressure valve before I became that nut job on the top of the bell tower with the high-powered rifle yelling as I picked people off, "All you had to do was make a reservation... one fucking reservation!"

In all the bubbling madness, however, my blog was born, and this electronic journal became not only my personal saving grace but, more important, yours. I got to go to work and be charmed or distraught with the human diner and then go home to regurgitate the evening onto the keyboard, not on your lovely evening with your wife or girlfriend (or both; I've seen it all). I got to go home and make light of the people and scenarios I was privy to without ever using a proper name. I began to therapeutically develop my understanding of the human interaction that takes place at a table during meal service and begin to cultivate philosophies about how to make your and my lives better places to eat in. I got to tell you all about yourself without you knowing it was about you.

But the most important thing I got to do was laugh out loud at the madness of it all. I am a huge proponent of "comedy for one," which to me is being able to make myself laugh even if it is at your expense. If you can't make yourself laugh, you'll never be able to make others even crack a smile. I truly believe that all parties involved are the better for it—or at least can potentially become so; we will see.

The Yacht Club

This venue was supposed to be my pinnacle. The top rung, the show. I was led to believe that I was accepting the position of general manager.

Let the record show that just because you get the owner of a restaurant begrudgingly to accept your salary demand, it does not make you more important in title or in fact. I would go so far as to say that I was even more the whipping boy here than at any previous workplace. I was "head" manager, meaning that my responsibility included keeping the daytime manager (my co-) interested in his job, despite the fact that the only thing he liked about it was his paycheck. He had been acting manager for many years and saw my arrival as his relief; he was all too glad to hand the neurotic reins of the owner over to me while he headed out on another bender with the staff after hours. While "daytime Dave" stepped back into the shadows from which he came, I got to sell myself to a whole new staff and clientele who had been together for double-digit years. I never fit right with anybody.

I spent one year here, and every day was utilized figuring out how to get off this merry-go-round industry before I slapped some retiree with a whole dead fish. Every day scheming how to say good-bye to mandatory wine tasting and oyster knowledge. While I was in awe of the longevity of the business, nothing else held my interest, and daily I would die a little more exiting the freeway headed to the clubhouse, never properly initiated.

Much more on this establishment in the section called "Bluer Pastures" in chapter 8.

CHAPTER 3

Not a Trained Philosopher

You Get "It" or You Don't

For the longest time I was truly unable to pinpoint the root of my growing frustration with some of the people whom I was so honored to serve and manage. On a macro level there were just far too many ingredients to truly boil it down to one underlying condition. It would be like tasting Aunt B's "all-day" collards and trying to pinpoint a hint of nutmeg... just not going to happen right away, until I started paying acute attention to every situation that tumbled down my turnpike instead of haphazardly dealing with situations as they arose, then dismissing them as momentary annoyances devoid of true meaning.

Then out of the blue one day when I least expected it, a defined "aha" moment—and all at once a theory of life struck me without warning! A theory that would carve out a niche of human understanding and most days become the bane of my existence: "You get it, or you don't."

On one of my many walks from the dining room to the kitchen with a "re-fire" (food sent back for being unacceptable), a flash of insight revealed to me this aforementioned philosophy.

The world is completely divided into two groups. There is no room for gray areas here. You either "get it" or you don't. I cannot overemphasize the word *completely* here. There is but one line drawn in the sand that has you standing on either this side, or that. No toes are creeping over. Here it is again... "You get it, or you don't."

What is "it," besides an improper word to use when writing anything with more meaning than a text message? "It" is every scenario we come into contact with every day that molds our worldview and the principles we live by. "It" is the very clay that becomes the shape of our character and how we conduct ourselves on a moment-to-moment basis. How we deal with situations as they arise based on past lessons and outcomes from behaviors. A karmic fingerprint that is unique to every individual on the planet. Among modern peoples, "it" was the fight-or-flight response, and *Seinfeld* made reference to "it" in scenes where the reactionary George Costanza pushed women and children out of the way en route to the door upon hearing the word "Fire!" But I have found that in our culture of dwindling patience, where brevity reigns supreme, it is best to call it "it." Here are a couple of examples from my personal experience that define "it" for me:

- People who know that lousy service still deserves a 15 percent tip get "it." People who use a coupon for a free meal and tip 10 percent on the discounted bill—don't.
- People who plan to include their teenage kids in their social activities in order to bond with them get "it." People who buy their teenage kids a keg so that "at least we know where they are drinking"—don't. (*Sidenote: true example from a bartender I hired later in life, a bartender I repeatedly had to police from watching the Home Shopping Network behind the bar during business hours. The very bartender who yelled to me one day over many bar patrons, "Toby... FYE... we are out of Stoli Limón." FYE? Really?*)

- People who order coffee for the end of their meal get "it." People who order hot tea—don't. (This phenomenon will most certainly be covered later.)
- People who try daring new menu items in the hopes of an expansive palate adventure and give their honest opinion to the server after paying the bill get "it." People who send their fish back because it tastes "fishy"—don't.

One of my favorite movies and movie quotes has Meg Ryan putting this phenomenon into the perfect word combination. "My father says that most of the world, almost everybody you see, is asleep, but the rest of us walk around in a constant state of amazement." *Joe versus the Volcano* gets "it."

The pressing question at hand, now that our vision has become so dramatically unobstructed, is when the shaping of "it" happens, and how we can all make sure that we fall onto the right side of the line. The element of nature versus nurture plays a huge role here, and many of us may have to unlearn years of advice from misguided parenting techniques. Just because you were born and raised in an aquarium of "don't get its" does not necessarily mean that you can't grow legs and walk your ass onto land; it will most likely just require a little more effort for you than others. Perhaps after an extended period of self-analysis, you feel comfortable that you have been paying close attention to your actions and reactions. You have compiled and crunched the data, but still an uncertainty looms above your desired brain. Certainly no preordained pontiff is going to emerge from the crowd and touch you with his scepter, allowing all those around you to know with certainly that you have been anointed as "getting it."

So when? When do you get the reassurance that you're one of the enlightened? When do you get to know if all your hard work at removing yourself from your parents' trailer-park mentality has paid off? When can you be reassured that Meg Ryan was referring to you in a positive light and you're not one of the sleeping ones? In a flash at a silent unknowable time, that's when. When you find yourself shopping for shampoo, or channel-surfing on your bed and dissecting another repeat of *Mythbusters,* and all at once your eyes thrust from their sockets, you sit straight up, and you exclaim to nobody in particular, "Holy shit... *I get it!*"

I suppose this could be a simple explanation of an unarguable point, and then again I suppose there could be some other processes and results yet to be determined, but the underlying point remains the same—you do or you don't, and I know because... *I get it!*

Perhaps It's the Weather

In my endless collecting of notes on management behavior I have observed factors that shape the mind-set at any given period of time. More often than not I am a professional mask wearer. "Shiny happy people holding hands," gumdrops and rainbows, sugar and spice and all these good things, my job suggests, nay, *requires* that I execute flawlessly. Please note that this by no stretch of imagination means that inside I am the live in a shanty in the woods, manifesto-writing, beard-growing mess that is the flip side of the aforementioned Michael Stipe lyric. I'm not—I am quite happy internally all twelve months of the year. Perhaps a little less so when customers complain that their "well-done" steak is overcooked, but hey, what can you do?

However, during a stretch of three months toward the end of each year I would feel like tearing my flesh open at the sternum and yelling at nobody in particular, "*Are you serious? Really?*" Most days during this season my patience is thin and the therapeutic rebel yell wants so badly to come pouring out.

After noting this phenomenon for a few years in a row I began to wonder if the onset of colder weather, which directly correlates to a surge in dining populations, might be a factor. We desire to the point of requiring more people spending their collective wealth in restaurants, and should relish this seasonal opportunity not only to turn a profit but just to stay in business, not to mention the all-important first impressions that can be made on the first-time diner in the hope that they will remember us in the summer. Regardless of how cluelessly 20 percent of diners may act, it should become the quest for the other 80 percent. I remind myself that unlike many other occupations, my cubicle came with a fully stocked bar, and that much like sex and pizza, even when it was bad, it was still pretty good; but still sometimes (not unlike so many of us) I just felt like screaming.

Could there be a direct link between inner angst and frosty pumpkins? The business seemed to be colorful and pleasurable to be around in June but closed and angry during the winter months. The company of fellow managers also in angry limbo and also in need of hibernation was adequate to keep the angst in check, and they served as a therapeutic sound board behind closed doors, but the daily vigilance required to prevent unnecessary and illogical reactions was certainly heightened. Bottom line is that you should cut a little more slack to those in the business around the holidays because we are busier than we are the rest of the year, our social lives are replaced by yours, and most important... we are cold. Come back in June to complain about your dry chicken—it is so much easier to tackle that issue in mental flip-flops.

CHAPTER 4

Reservations

Single-handedly, the seemingly inconsequential making of the reservation, or failure to do so, has shown itself to be the greatest single thorn in my side and created its own boundaries and definitions consistently throughout my time in the trenches. The importance of a first impression can't be overstated. And the act of making a reservation is exactly that. This is the very first impact that an individual could possibly have on a future dining experience—so much so that if this obligatory gesture is cast aside with as little thought as "they'll have room, we'll just walk in," you are already starting your evening on step two... not good for all parties involved.

Let's begin by breaking down the actual word *reservation*. The first part of the word is "reserve," as in setting aside an appropriate-size table to accommodate any persons attending the impending dinner or lunch extravaganza. (*Sidenote: you never have to make a reservation for breakfast unless it is a special-occasion brunch such as Mother's Day or Easter.*) This aspect alone is crucial to the outcome of any social gathering, regardless of how large or small you may interpret your party size to be.

However, the unsung importance of the reservation lies in the root of the second part of the word, "-ation," as in, "preparation." This, to the staff of the chosen dining place, is as "reserve" is to the guests. In layman's terms—you the guest "reserve" a table and we the staff prepare it.

So you see, the word itself is a complete representation of the role of all parties involved in the execution of the perfect evening, and without it you are running the severe risk of jeopardizing the visual fantasy of the perfect evening you had in mind. And for the love of Mike, don't you dare complain to me that it has taken your waitress/hostess ten minutes to recognize your existence when you came in off the street with seven other people! Thirty other assholes did the same thing about ten minutes ago and she is a little busy; however, had we known you were coming, you could already have been sipping on your Cosmos and nibbling on your calamari. Perhaps next time you will let us know that your family reunions annual dinner is today and you would like to know if 7:30 would be okay.

Confused? Let us put it in a practical, and all too common, scenario.

Saturday 6:30 P.M. (peak hour of operations)

"Good evening and thank you for calling ___, this is Toby. How can I help you?"

"Yeah—do we need a reservation?"

"Yes, they are strongly suggested. What time would you like to come in?" (Let the record show that this question is executed with a congenial smile, because although the question cuts to the core of any reputable restaurant, I really have no way of knowing if this person is an asshole or not *yet*).

"I dunno, around seven-thirty."

"I believe I might be able to squeeze you in. How many in your party?" (Smile is getting tighter as phone guest rapidly approaches asshole status. *Dumb question + peak hour request = possible asshole.* Beware!)

"Oh. Okay, Let's see: 1, 2, 3, 4, 5, 6, 7... I think there's like fourteen of us."

Total asshole!

At this point the smile is über-tight, my teeth are grinding, and I continue: "Why don't you come in for a predinner beverage in the lounge, and I'll see what I can do about a table for you and your party of 'like fourteen,' but it may be closer to eight-thirty. Your last name, Sir?"

This is where management jobs are lost, people cry, and a judge to be named later orders those anger management courses I referred to earlier. I not only liked my job, I needed it—and no judge was going to tell me whom to hang out with for six months while I worked on my issues!

It's 6:30 P.M. on a Saturday and you and thirteen of your closest Mensa think-tank companions just decided that you wanted dinner, in one hour, at a linen and wineglass restaurant, and you start the phone call with "Do we need a reservation?" If I could reach through the phone and perform a vasectomy or perhaps rip out your ovaries to prevent future generations of helmet-wearing droolers like you from dining out, so help me God, I would.

Even if the desired dining time happened to be a Tuesday at 4:30 P.M. and the restaurant was completely empty, I still might hang up on this person on principle alone. "No, of course, Sir, let me just erase four of these other reservations for people who called a week ago, to make some room for you and your super-important guests."

What exactly are they expecting to hear? And do they get mad and shocked when you say there is no possible way we could accommodate such a large group at that time? Oh, you betcha!

You see, to "reserve" space (of any size) takes prepare-"ation." So please—for the love of all things holy—give your favorite places at least twenty-four hours' notice of your visit, even if you're dining alone or if you just decided to go to "that place" you read about but you're sure that it's not fancy enough to need a reservation, hear my voice reminding you: it's not all about you, and you are not always right. Don't be a potential asshole, and call (even if it's from the car in front of the building) and ask if it's okay to come in. This philosophy is not intended to elevate my elitisms; it is simply to provide the best possible experience for you and your company.

Another major point of the art of reservations has become strikingly apparent in the wake of the country's recent economic downturn. The old way used to be that restaurants could staff the hell out of a floor with as many servers as desired for optimal standards to be reached. Not unlike many other aspects of the shifting nature of F&B, this practice has given way to frugality. The minimum-wage employees who are there to practice their craft do so with the acute knowledge that they pay their rent by the generosity of others, and the $8.00 an hour that they earn from the company is paid only so that the government doesn't look out the corner of its eye in their direction. Most professional fine-dining servers use their hourly-wage paycheck merely to cover the cost of taxes on the tips they report. If they could, they would show up for free, and more often than not, servers forget that they even have a paycheck (or six) waiting for them in the office. It's a wash.

So back in the days of wine and roses, a manager could have ten servers on staff for forty expected guests and not blink an eye if only the Friday and Saturday crowds were providing enough business to create a successful restaurant. If nothing else, this attention to detail would make the manager's job easier. But today we mangers walk a fine line. When I come in to work three hours before service starts, the first task at hand is to look at the books (reservations) and see how many people are coming in. If there are twenty-four reservations and I have four servers on, best believe that I am sending somebody home. Every cent counts nowadays when running the floor.

Now at 7:00 P.M. with just the right ratio of workers to diners for that symbiotic dance to take place, asshole after asshole files in the door without a reservation and totally weeds my staff. So

weeded are they that I myself have to roll up the sleeves to my
dress shirt, break out my tie chain to keep from trailing it in your
soup, and start hustling plates back and forth yelling things like
"Clear twenty, I've got entrées dying in the window," and "Has
anybody been to 62?... Oh, I guess I'll start it," or, my favorite as
a manager, which the rest of the staff is never allowed to yell to
the bartenders or kitchen: "Verbal ordering one Manhattan and
two Rombauer Chards... I'll ring it later."

God forbid that the kitchen has done the unthinkable and
undercooked your steak, because you're not getting hold of a
manger tonight to rectify the problem; I am too busy garnishing
Old-Fashioneds and explaining which oysters are which to table
14. This might make the attention-starved diner distraught to
the point of anger, but through clenched teeth and a pursed
smile, let me remind you that it was you who decided to "walk
in" unannounced with six of your closest friends.

The rule of thumb has changed as well. Back at the beginning
of my career, reservations were almost an exact science. That is
to say, if I looked at the books at 3:00 P.M. and saw fifty-six
people were planning on joining us that evening, I could count
on perhaps sixty to sixty-four total at the end of the night. Please
allow me to pause and gaze glowingly upward in fond
remembrance of those times. We call those the "salad years"...
okay, I'm back, but those days of yore are a distant dream. Now
when I come in at 3:00 P.M. and see fifty people, I instinctively
add a 100 percent to 150 percent increase in covers—meaning that
I can be assured that we will do up to 150 dinners that evening.

I cannot begin to tell you how frightening this trend is. If my
math is correct, then within ten years reservation tools like
OpenTable or even the paper and pencil (never pen—nothing in
F&B is that permanent) will be housed in restaurant museums
where field-trip kids will gawk on a Wednesday afternoon at the
ancient artifacts used by hostesses of the past. In short—please

make a reservation. There is no reason we can't come together collectively to stop the bleeding; but unfortunately I cannot make the first move. The ball's in your court, McEnroe, so do the right thing and make both of our experiences as positive as we know they can be.

St. Valentine's Day Massacre

Not making reservations during the week and even during the weekend aside, there are times where even the lowliest of Cro-Magnon man should be able to wrap his mind around the necessity of making a reservation.

It has never ceased to amaze me how a date on the calendar, of all things, can sneak up on a person, but every February 14 a slew of people flood the phone lines at the last minute to try to appease potential angry partners with a last-minute reservation at their favorite fine-dining spot. My restaurants have never been an exception to this, and part of me relishes the opportunity to expose these unprepared patrons of fine dining.

To their credit and my entertainment, some people sprinkle their desperation with a smattering of creativity in the hopes that we may take the reservation without ever noticing that it is our busiest day of the year.

"Thank you for calling, this is Toby, how can I help you?"

"I would like to get a reservation for Saturday around seven-thirty."

"The fourteenth?"

"Yes."

"Valentine's Day?"

"Oh! Is that Valentine's Day?"

"Nice try, Sir, we have been booked solid for two months. Looks like another Valentine's Day has snuck up on you again, but good luck with your special night of Domino's pizza and masturbation as your wife/girlfriend/ boyfriend / whatever will be too angry with you to touch you. I hear there is a good skin flick on Max."

The modern calendar was adopted in Pope Gregory's time in the sixteenth century. You have no excuse to be surprised by a holiday that requires reservations.

The other anomaly that fascinates me more is how empowered people think they are because they want to spend money.

"Happy Valentine's Day, this is Toby, how can I help you?"

"I would like a reservation tonight at eight."

"I'm sorry, Sir, but we have been booked solid for two months. Can I put you on the imaginary wait list that, if it actually existed, would be as long as the Washington Monument is high and offer absolutely no chance of entry into the building tonight?"

"You mean to tell me that you are going to turn down my business in this economy?" (Oh, boy—here we go. This particular, but in no way unique, individual has tipped his hand that he is in no uncertain terms "that guy." (More on "that guy" later.)

"No, Sir, I am telling you that I am *happy* to turn down your business, because it just occurred to me that if you were here tonight, I am positive you would find a way to send your food back, complain about your table assignment, and tell me to turn up the heat because you are more important than the other three hundred people in the restaurant. Pardon me, but you just sound like that kind of an ass. I am looking forward to our annual conversation next February fourteenth. Talk to you then. Have a good year!"

Please, people—heed my advice. February 14 is Valentine's Day, and it falls directly between the thirteenth and fifteenth every year, never changes. This day requires a nice romantic meal for you and your partner, and therefore a reservation. Most restaurants can take reservations up to a year in advance. So eat your romantic meal, pay your check, and then stop at the host stand for your mint or toothpick and make your reservation for 365 days in the future—if for no other reason than so I don't have to talk to you next year at the zero hour.

This advice works just as well for Mother's Day, Easter, Christmas Eve, New Year's Eve, and the Fourth of July, all holidays that fall into the Holy Grail category in F&B.

As George W. Bush would say, "It's not rocket surgery, folks."

CHAPTER 5

Employee - Guest Dynamics

If the restaurant is a wheel, then the two types of spokes are the employees and the guests. To delve a little deeper, one could imagine the hub as the owners and the managers as the tire. This implies that the tire is still a tire without any help from the spokes and the hub is the reason that we are all there, but the spokes make it a wheel and the two types of spokes exist in dynamic alternation—that is to say, guest, employee, guest, employee, guest, employee, and so on in the grand scheme of the restaurant cycle.

I was taught early in my career to not refer to the person who comes to spend money at your establishment as a customer. That label seems to be so 1950s McDonald's. That person is instead a guest and should be treated as such. Managers use visualization as a valuable tool for training the staff, and painting the mental imagery of the dining room as your personal home and all who enter it as meaningful guests helps to assure some semblance of politeness in the tap dance that is food service.

You should always maintain a pleasant exterior, even if your world is silently crashing around you. As a server that means that even if your girlfriend left you and when you were leaving the house that day you inadvertently backed out over your dog, killing him instantly, less than ten minutes before you arrived for your shift, your expressions and demeanor should suggest that you are one of (if not the) happiest person on the planet and lack any problems to speak of. You can cry in your shift beer later. In addition, make sure that you yourself, or somebody else, is at the door to thank the guests upon their exit. If you were throwing a dinner party at your personal abode and these "guests" who are there now were the people on your invitee list, it would be unthinkable to be in the bathroom when they left your house with no form of recognition from you, the host. No different at the restaurant. Yes, there are hired hostesses who have that responsibility firmly written in their job description—to be at the front at all times of service ready to welcome guests and thank them upon their exit—but one should never assume that they will be there at the appropriate time (hostesses have an uncanny ability to wander away at optimal moments).

The key is to grasp firmly the fact that while it was nice for these people to come by and help you make your rent this month, it is more important that they tell their friends around the water cooler the next day what a wonderful time they had and how beautiful your home was, thereby ensuring that they return to do it all again soon.

Conversely, the guest should have certain responsibilities as well, but of course, these are completely unmanageable by hired staff. These rules and points of etiquette should be implied by (one hopes) your proper upbringing, but they cannot possibly be relied upon or altered. Does being invited to a dinner party at a private home empower a person so much as to test the boundaries of service? I think not, yet this phenomenon happens all the time at a restaurant. Have you ever wandered into a person's home and before you have even removed your coat suggested the proper air-conditioning and music settings to the host? Again, probably not, or at least I hope not; so therefore you should not attempt to do these things at any sit-and-pay establishment.

As staff we are all elated that you came to join us and will do our best to make sure you are comfortable and your wallets stay nice and loose—our basic cable packages and Xbox 360s waiting for us at our studio apartments depend on it—but please do us the courtesy of dishing out some benefit of the doubt that we are (for the most part) professionals and are good at our craft. Unless of course you have decided to dine at the lunch counter in your local hospital or are picking up a grilled cheese sandwich between sessions at the blackjack table in Vegas, in which case feel free to fart audibly and blame the waitress. That is not the arena I'm talking about.

A Little Ditty

As a manager who believes in, but does not particularly love, conducting lineups, I am constantly looking for tutorials to offer the staff in the form of handouts and worksheets. These materials have two advantages. The first is that they keep our daily message fresh. Attempting to hold the attention of every server for fifteen minutes a day is challenging enough, but throw into the mix actually reaching them and motivating them to go out and be the best damned earners they can be for the restaurant and not merely themselves is like teaching Chinese algebra to an elephant. The second is that most everything that can be said to motivate has probably been said before by somebody else and more eloquently at that, so handouts are valuable (usually).

The following little ditty is something that was handed to me prior to one lineup by one of the many owners I have had the pleasure of working with, one who spent gobs of time scouring the Internet for tools to arm the troops with. I was handed the document just before the lineup started, so I was unable to peruse it prior to reading it aloud to the staff. As I heard the words for the first time, I became increasingly aware of the whore I was painting myself out to be and the example I was asking my staff to follow. The document was a generalized version of the perspective of a person who might be thinking of eating with us at some point in the future, but it became the very essence of what I have so pointedly become averse to about some guests... their sense of entitlement.

"I Am Your Guest"

You often accuse me of carrying a chip on my shoulder, but I suspect this is because you do not entirely understand me. Isn't it normal to expect satisfaction for one's money spent? Ignore my wants and I will no longer appear in your restaurant. Satisfy those wants and I will become increasingly loyal. Add a little extra personal attention and a friendly touch and I will become a walking advertisement for you.

When I criticize your food and service to anyone who will listen, which I may do whenever I am displeased, take heed. I am not dreaming up displeasure. It lies in something I perceive you have failed to do to make my eating experience as enjoyable as I have anticipated. Eliminate that perception or you will lose my friends and me as well. I insist on the right to dine leisurely or eat in haste according to my mood.

I refuse to be rushed as much as I abhor waiting. This is an important privilege that my money buys. If I am not spending big money this particular time, just remember, if you treat me right I will return with a larger appetite, more money, and probably with my friends.

I am much more sophisticated these days than I was just a few years ago. I've grown accustomed to better things, and my needs are more complex. I'm perfectly willing to spend, but I insist on quality to match prices. I am, above all, a human being. I am especially sensitive when I am spending money. I can't stand to be snubbed, ignored, or looked down upon.

Whatever my personal habits may be, you can be sure that I'm a real nut on cleanliness in restaurants. Where food is concerned I demand the strictest sanitation measures. I want my meals handled and served by the neatest of people and in sparkling clean dishes. If I see dirty fingernails, cracked dishes, or soiled tablecloths, you won't see me again.

You must prove to me again and again that I have made a wise choice in selecting your restaurant above others. You must convince me repeatedly that being a restaurant guest is a desirable thing in the first place. I can, after all, eat at home. So you must provide something extra in food and service. Something so superior it will beckon me from my own table to yours. Do we understand each other?

In my most humble opinion, even the lay reader at this point should feel just a bit filthier than before reading that swill. I truly believe that this tutorial should have been (and possibly was originally) written by carefully cutting out different letters from magazines and placing them together in a patchwork just like any other professional ransom note. Let it be known that I was handed the printed copy only, with no envelope information whatsoever, and let it also be known that this lack of information on the author's identity probably saved the person's life or, if nothing else, a good toilet papering and lawn bleaching. In short, *fuck this guy!* (*Sidenote: it helps me to picture the author as a guy so I don't feel like a jerk with so much rage against a woman.*)

I love the "you must repeatedly prove to me" part. Why? If we have proved it once, then go ahead and expect it again. I get a guttural chuckle out of my mental image of the dude writing this. I see him as the James Earl Jones character in *Coming to America* as his holiness travels to New York to retrieve his son and is constantly disappointed with the lack of attention paid to his presence. The author of this particular ode must certainly have been royalty in another country, as he is so comfortable telling us minions to bow before him. I can't believe that he didn't find the time to tell us not to make eye contact and to chew his food for him.

This opinionated piece (of shit) basically told my staff to be hookers to his pimpness, and I'll be damned if I'll ever instill that sort of lesson into any of the people I manage. It all boils down to this: if the staff members enjoy what they do, that enjoyment will be passed on to the diner. Have you ever seen anybody enjoy being bitch-slapped in public because your soup was merely hot, not piping?

On a rudimentary level, the author has some valid points, and let us not forget that we are all there to hone our professional craft in the hopes for repeat business, but the fact that his ego steps in the way and creates a six-paragraph ultimatum cheapens his intended message. To this douche and the others who nod their heads in agreement while reading his manifesto, I say, good day and please don't let the door hit you where the good Lord split you, as you are not welcome here. I said, *good day, Sir!*

Needless to say, I spent a good portion of that evening going to each server who had to sit through my Teddy Ruxpin recitation of that material to apologize individually for possibly making them dumber and hoping that as a team we could move forward and allow me to retain some shred of credibility. I never did see whether the damage was irreparable.

The Other Side of the Coin

Staying on the subject of lineups and the endless handouts given as tools to help the staff by the micromanaging owner, the very day after I had puked the aforementioned ode to Mr. High and Mighty, I was given the passage that follows. This was from a study done at Cornell University and published in its *Hospitality Quarterly*. It was a snapshot of key practices that promoted guest retention and repeat business. The two-page report was clear, concise, but too detailed for the short attention spans of your average service personnel, but at the end it broke down the thirteen key practices proved to be the most effective ways to enhance the dining experience for guest and server alike. I share with you now those steps; the comments in parenthesis are my personal take on each.

1   The server wore or carried something unusual *(flair is for TGIFridays, but I'm all for a conversation piece like a necklace or obsidian earrings)*.

2   Introduced yourself by name to your guests *(so important to me; our mothers gave us names for a reason)*.

3   Tried suggestive selling.

4   Squatted next to the table or sat at the table when interacting with guests *(this is an old child development trick to get onto eye level; status and hierarchy can be unintentionally implied by an elevated eye level)*.

5   Touched your guests *(careful here: this means on the shoulder. For the love of Pete, do not squish their cheeks or fondle their earlobes)*.

6   Told your guests stories or jokes *(stay away from "A Jew, a Catholic nun, and a whore walk into a bar ...")*.

7   Repeated guests' orders back to them when they were ordering *(this is a warm fuzzy that allows guests to be reassured that you are paying attention to them)*.

8   Called your guests by their names *(it shows that you retained the information they shared with you in step 2)*.

9   Drew pictures on your guests' checks *(I'm not a huge fan of this one, but if you must, make it simple—a smiley face or sun, no Bart Simpson doodles or caricatures)*.

10   Gave your customers big open-mouth smiles *(a good reason to not eat on shift)*.

11   Wrote "Thank you" on the back of the guests' checks *(this should replace pictures, don't do both)*.

12 Told your guests if the weather forecast for the next day is favorable or good *(notice they left out the option for crappy weather)*.

13 Complimented your guests on their food selection *(again—brilliant: everybody wants validation for making the right decisions in life, even if it's just a seafood risotto)*.

One of the fascinating things about this study is that it encompasses every sort of eatery. These practices can be followed from the greasy spoon to the white-linen places and should be practiced on a regular basis. The whole key to success in any situation is to simplify and recognize the fact that we are all just humans sharing space on the same terra firma. No one person is better or worse, we all just come with a different set of circumstances.

So the key to success for the individual and the establishment is perception at its most rudimentary level. As a guest or employee, do not perceive yourself to be more than you are. The fact is that unless you have developed the ability to fly or superhuman strength, you are not more than anybody else on the planet, and besides, the smell of bullshit carries farther than the scent of flowers, giving the opposing party that much more time to prepare for your arrival.

I Have Been to the Top of the Mountain and the View Was Amazing

Most food writers, in an attempt to establish credibility, have at one time or another paid verbal homage to the master, Thomas Keller. He runs an operation that leaves anybody in the business breathless and at a loss to duplicate. Long ago I believed that he set a bar that should be aspired to by anybody in the business, and while that claim has not necessarily been disproved, it has become eroded by the asterisks that have been added with experience.

Quite simply, he has been done to death, but I am here to tell you that it is because the experience he creates needs to be talked about. There is just no other way. His talent and the attention to detail practiced by his people in every facet of the business should not necessarily be emulated when the proverbial shoe does not fit. If you are a Denny's franchisee and read one of Mr. Keller's books or even visit one of his restaurants, you would be ill advised to go back to your restaurant and have a young French boy describing word for word the fourteen-course tasting menu of the night. Every place has its identity and should be constructed with respect for that identity. For me, though, being subjected to the world of fine dining and having the firsthand experience of a Thomas Keller establishment allowed me to understand exactly what heights could be achieved. His level of service is not Sasquatchian, it does exist, and is very real.

The second I heard tales of the French Laundry in Yountville I called the restaurant as your average citizen and made a standing reservation. Sounds easy, huh? The fact is that I remained on a waiting list for three years. So long, in fact, that when they finally called to say I had a table for four at six the following Friday, I had no recollection of what they were talking about. I declined, and thanked them very much for their unwavering tenacity.

At various times in my career, I would be subtly reminded of just how important it was for me to experience that level of the game. True to the adage "it's all who you know," one day I was lucky enough to be offered the chance to join six of the people most dear to me on the planet, including my onetime food and beverage mentor and now closest compadre, Juliann, at a table for seven on the hallowed grounds. This time I would not forget the approaching date as it was only a month away.

Contrary to anybody's beliefs about my personal state of mind, I am not solely a jaded, chip-on-the-shoulder elitist who takes valuable time out of his day to unload bags of semantic waste on the industry that chose me as a member. Within every unwanted and seemingly indigestible plate of brussels sprouts and boiled cabbage, there always lies the promise of an ice cream sundae or piece of pecan pie as a reward. (Let the record show I actually enjoy brussels sprouts and boiled cabbage, but one cannot escape the iconic image of the undesirable when using these timeless examples.) This day at The French Laundry was to be a crescendo in the form of the single best dining experience of my career!

I speak lovingly so as to do justice to the sheer gastronomical heights achieved by this sleepy little cottage in Yountville called The French Laundry, accented so appropriately with the perfectly cast table of characters. In attendance for this carnival for carnivores were some of my most cherished inhabitants of the Earth from all generations and all walks of life. All of them not only shared in, but overwhelmingly relished in appreciation our four-hour dining experience. Oohs and ahhs abound!

The exterior of The French Laundry in Yountville is like a Thomas Kinkade painting. You know the place: cozy brick-laden cottage with wonderfully historic old gnarled trees wrapping around the front of the façade, multipaned windows that allow just a peek into the candlelit kitchen from the manicured front lawn, not big enough to pitch a large camping tent on. Inviting to say the least, and it really does give the visceral feeling that a fluffy bunny should be quietly singing with a wise old frog somewhere in the garden.

Suffice it to say that I will not be reliving the marathon meal ingredient by ingredient, but rather touching on the aspects that set this place apart from all others—like the servers in full pressed suits that were clinically clean. No traces of last night's sweat on the cuffs of these pros, and all three buttons up the front of their suit jackets fastened fastidiously, accenting the perfect Windsor knot under a starched collar... and her name was Shannon!

Allowing us to select between the left-side nine-course chef's tasting menu or the right-side nine-course chef's tasting menu (both $240.00 U.S., tax and tip included), she sidled up to the table and warmly greeted us before reciting from memory every word from both sides of said menu, with extra descriptors. (Reader, be aware that these menus are completely different every day, so the flawless execution of this task is a monumental feat of memory.)

At four points in the nine-course meal, we the consumers are forced to make a decision between two items, such as the sautéed fillet of Columbia River sturgeon or the sashimi of Japanese hamachi, and the sirloin of Devils Gulch Ranch rabbit "en persillade" or the moulard (not mallard) duck foie gras "en terrine"... you get the idea.

Shortly after we made our decisions, she vanished, and was to be seen again only twice during the meal itself and then constantly at the end. The rest of the duties were turned over to her more than capable support crew. I will refrain now and forever from calling these people runners, bussers, or expos because those names their craft no justice.

Throughout the next four-plus hours, plates were placed from the left using the left hand in synchronized service right under your nose, and silently. Really—you looked down and there was food, and you wondered, "How the hell did that get there?" as a flash of black blazer ducked down the stairs just out of the corner of your eye. Once placed to perfection, an adorable little French man (no more than twenty years old) arrived and with a heavy French accent and the precision of a surgeon explained what was in front of you. (Also flawless.) Let the "Oh my God"s and the "Can you believe this" followed by the occasional "There are no words," ensue, but never, *I mean never*, any "Holy shits" or "Jesus Christ"s (this isn't the place, as much as you want to scream them). And it was this way until the last morsel and sip of hot coffee vanished from existence.

This type of eating is art. It is so much more than food and beverage service. It is religion.

The evening started very quiet with everyone sitting with perfect posture conversing about world travel and books we were reading, but it ended with voice volume raised above clinking silverware and conversation about Kool-Aid and nakedness, not unlike the way any successful and appreciated meal should dictate what a wonderful time one is having.

While this particular experience has now been checked off my bucket list, like anything a person thoroughly enjoys, the idea of a potential second helping is salivated over. Rest assured that while I could never use my time there as a bar for the standards my own restaurant should achieve, you can bet that I will roll my eyes and feel a little more defeated the next time one of my own forgets to put a steak knife down before the entrée course or asks out loud to anybody who will answer, "What is al dente?"

CHAPTER 6

Staff

A Note to Applicants

Step one in becoming part of what so many restaurants consider a "family," not merely staff, is applying for the job. Not unlike many other forms of seeking employment, there are guidelines that should be followed, but for some reason, the ne'er-do-well applicant typically butchers the process when it comes to F&B— so much so that managers like myself have learned warning signs to watch out for.

One of the driving factors in this hiccup of moral conduct is the freshly open floodgates of the unemployed. In the recent past the nation has seen an incredible rise in the stable becoming unstable, and no arena of employment can be considered safe. The six-figure executive with the picture-perfect life, the auto mechanic who years ago accepted that his lot in life was to not necessarily be "a lot in life" but just enough, the schoolteacher who was relying on tenure but came up just short, and the salesman who was left with a pink slip and a suitcase full of hotel shower rings have all entered the unimagined ranks of the unemployed.

Funny thing about jobs and security—they can leave so abruptly but the bills never do. I imagine all these poor souls lying awake at 3:00 A.M., when the mind is a playground full of sharp corners and broken glass, trying desperately to figure out how they are going to keep a roof over their family's head. More often than not, it would seem, the comforting thought that allows them to drift off for just one more night of blissful slumber is the memory that they worked the deli counter in college thirty years ago, so the next day they will go door-to-door to all the eating establishments in their area and find gainful employment in an industry that most certainly will be glad to have them back.

I feel partly ashamed to admit that for the past couple of years, a great source of entertainment behind the scenes for management has been poring over recently submitted applications and résumés. From the high school kids who are trying to break in for the first time to the aforementioned desperate who are trying to rekindle the glory days of cash in hand, the copious accounts of qualifications splattered with grammatical errors have come to provide anticipated fodder for many a closed-door laugh riot. My intent is not to turn a person down for trying; by all means it should be noted that we rely heavily on the arsenal of desirables to choose from when there is a shift in our internal structure. My intent here is to shed a little light on how not to be the source of amusement for those privy to reading your résumé and how to go about maximizing your chances of getting past the front door, let alone a sit-down meeting with me or my co-s. This may seem dramatically harsh, but believe you me, many applicants have been shot down and their résumé "round-filed" (thrown away) before they have even made it out of the parking lot.

Lesson one: a note about the phone. In this day of heightened communications all people should at least grasp the concept of how powerful the phone is and can be. Against the grain of common belief, I am not solely referring to the masses lucky enough to have an iPhone, unlimited texting, and any number of other "personal" communication devices. I am reaching back to the days of yore that cling to today like a child to their binky unable to grasp what life would be like without the security of the good ol'-fashioned landline. Named so because of the necessary unwavering support of the wall it is connected to, this device is still the backbone of any food service operation. Not so far back mind you as the archaic rotary-dial monster that had every person on the globe cursing individuals with the number 0 in their identifying phone number, but the go-to push-button phone, sometimes even in the form of a cordless device. This technological link to the outside world can be your most trusted ally in the art of the first impression, and in the same breath the mallet that drives the final nail in your coffin when in search of gainful employment. Here then are some dos and don'ts.

Please do call in advance and speak respectfully to whoever answers the phone. Have your script prepared in advance, for most people in the business have little time or patience for the "um, uhhhhh, I I I I" fillers.

"I am in the process of applying for employment at your company and I was wondering if I might get the name of the manager I should ask for when I come in later this week. And would it be possible for me to make an appointment with that person?"

There is nothing wrong with flowery language even if you don't use it on a regular basis. You will certainly get more hits with "Pardon me, Sir" than with "Dude, check this out." This is an example of sheer respectful professionalism, and I for one, if answering the phone that day, would give such persons my utmost time and tutelage. I may even go so far as to inquire about their name and dog-ear them mentally so that I put a name to the face when they arrive.

Most of the people who are even thinking about calling do the exact opposite. Do not call with the attitude that this is just another something to check off your list so that the unemployment officer assigned to your case may be appeased that you are actively seeking employment, when all you really want to do is stay in your mom's basement devoid of any natural light and play *World of Warcraft* all day. We have an innate sense for detecting these types of shenanigans.

"Yeah—are you guys hiring?"

Again, if answering the phone that day, I may again ask such people their name so that I will definitely remember it in the hope that they will come in, if for no other reason than to give me the therapeutic opportunity to round-file their paperwork. Most likely, though, said possible applicant will get a resounding "No, we are not hiring," and the matter will be given as little thought as the caller obviously put into dialing in the first place.

Lesson two: Regardless of how old you are or what your past successes have been, rest on the fact that we don't know you from Adam, so dress the part that you are seeking. If you treat it like "just a serving gig," you are demeaning what we do and showing firsthand the lack of respect you have for yourself. Don't even open your car door if you are wearing ripped skinny jeans, a loose sweater off the shoulder, visible tattoos, an Ed Hardy T-shirt (or any T-shirt for that matter), sneakers with stains, hair covering one eye, a loosened tie betraying quitting time at your "real job," or any number of inappropriate jewelry or cologne/perfume debacles.

Keep in mind that nicer restaurants have a titled position and workstation that puts a person in the front of the restaurant staring at the parking lot. During shift these people are called hosts or hostesses, but in downtimes they are watchdogs, and they can spot a wrinkled-résumé-wielding, down-on-their-luck, frown-wearing potential applicant from two hundred yards out.

Chances are great that they have already rung the office to warn me before you have even practiced your opening line. Dress like a professional and you will be treated like one. No matter how many other places you have been to that day convince the person, without words, that this restaurant is the only place you want to work, and by golly, you're happy just to be talking to somebody who already does.

Lesson three: Write your application and update your résumé with only pertinent information applicable to the position that you are seeking. That is to say, in ink (I can't believe that I have to write that but I do), list only what other F&B experience you have had and how long you were at said establishment. Unlike other employment sectors, in F&B multiple jobs and areas of practice do not hinder your quest, but rather help your chances. We like to see a broad scope of experience. We know it is rare for any "foodie" to be at one establishment for more than two years, so don't try to doctor this up. Conversely, we don't like to see that you have had fifteen foodie jobs in the past three years, but we can talk about that in an interview.

That right there is the point. Put the practical stuff on the surface, and we will dig up the "in between" times at a sit-down interview. I don't need to know right off the bat that you were a Xerox copy machine salesman and an HR representative for a hat manufacturer; that's not going to sell wine. I do need to know that you can interpret s.o.s. on a ticket for FF and a steak Oscar-style MR or find me a ramekin on a b&b with an under liner stat. Let's talk about rebuilding carburetors later.

Lesson four: Choose your visiting time very carefully. Do not mentally schedule your mythical appointment with a manager solely when it suits you. Take into consideration the potential schedule of the person you want to talk to. Restaurants have roughly the same operating schedules—lunchtime and dinnertime. These are not times to come cold-calling and expect to get a sit-down interview, or even make an impression other than that you are a douchebag who can't tell time... "Round-file that for me, will ya?"

Are we as managers to believe that you have made it this far in life without ever eating lunch or dinner? Of course not, so quickly before you leave the house, look at the clock: if it is between noon and 3:00 P.M., it's not your window and even worse, if it is after 5:00 P.M., you're out of luck for the day. Remember these times; they are imperative to your first impression. When I am running to a table to serve an armful of plates and a hostess stops me to tell me, "Ryan Smith is here to see you," I have to mentally scroll through my daily schedule while I peer up at the clock and respond at the same time, "Who is he?" By that time I am already hoping that she doesn't come back with "He is dropping off an application and would like to speak with you," because at that very minute, I already hate Ryan Smith and I don't even know him. I not only hate Ryan Smith, I want to punch his mom in her baby maker so that she doesn't create any more Ryan Smiths who may come by and apply for a job at 7:30 in the evening.

The long and short of the situation is, you're dead in the water. On two occasions I have actually followed potential applicants out the door as they were in the courtyard between my restaurant and the one next door for their second hit during the lunch rush, and stopped them for a quick tutorial. "Hey, Ryan, come here a minute. Here's the deal. I don't even know you but I want to give you some valuable advice so that you can help your chance of success in this business going forward. Clearly you don't know what I'm about to tell you, so my hope is that after today, you don't forget. Never go into a restaurant during operational hours of a meal. You blew it with me, but you don't have to blow it again next door." Both times Ryan has seemed receptive to my advice and the glimmer of knowledge seemed to be passed successfully, and both times I heard the door of the restaurant next door close as I walked away, as Ryan stepped knowingly into the next firing line. So much for my ability to teach, I should just stop while I'm only a little behind.

Jenna's Little Black Rain Cloud

At any given moment and on every night that the restaurant is open for business, it operates on a rail. This invisible, yet nonetheless very real, train track applies to every server, bartender, line cook, hostess, and busboy and, yes, even the managers on an individual basis unique to their own pre-constructed foundations. Every employee's personal rail is their responsibility, and the maintenance of this invisible factor can set them up for success or immediate failure. The individuals rail is automatically thwarted and tweaked the minute they step onto the floor still struggling with a hangover from the night before (a common occurrence in this business) or having gotten too little, or no, sleep the night before.

Yes, it is true that servers only work five-hour shifts on average, but the labor and intensity during that shift is no different from any other individual's nine-hour day in any other arena. The shift is fast-paced and full of unforeseen twists and turns. The comparison could be drawn between cubicleville's nice, leisurely bike ride along the coast versus the restaurant's fire-suit-wearing NASCAR race. This is a business that requires stamina and high thresholds for physical pain.

To return to the phenomenon of "tracks": once anything happens to derail a person during a shift, it becomes that much more difficult or impossible as time progresses to set the train right and get the evening back on its intended course. It would be like trying to untangle a knotted reel of fishing line after it not only has been cast but has a six-hundred-pound marlin on the other end. As noted, though, and because tracks are unique to each individual, more often than not, when a person jumps the track most of the people around them get to be thoroughly entertained as spectators. In a NASCAR crash, one man's horror becomes everyone else's entertainment. Conversely, any employee's derailment becomes the immediate responsibility of the floor managers as well, as we get involved to try to hoist the heavy machine back into place to salvage any tableside or clerical mistakes, which we will only have to fix in the future.

I have gone out of my way to keep all the people I write about anonymous, for better or worse, but when the evening I am about to describe transpired, I went immediately to my friend and employee Jenna and point-blank said, "Your night tonight made the book, and I am going to use your real name"—if for no other reason than the personal sickness that got me into this business, and the same one that kept me here year after year, just thought that this particular debacle was far to adorably tame not to document.

At this point it goes without saying that I had a server on staff named Jenna. She is one of the most delightful people I know. Never short of a smile, never profane, always polite. Every bit the lady parents hope their kids will become or find to marry. However, being the eternal optimist does not exclude you from the type of day Jenna had at the restaurant on the night in question. This being a perverse industry, one could make the argument that the foodie gods seek mousy characters like Jenna to throw their curveballs at more regularly than they seek the more rampant screw-up who is chock-full of bad life decisions. Those people have already been knocked around by life, so what's the challenge in that? It's the Jennas they are after, and that put my Jenna directly in the restaurant gods' crosshairs.

As the Nigerian-born author, Achebe, once wrote, "Things fall apart."

At first glance and from a distance, one would see only Jenna's pressed uniform accompanied by her delightfully multicolored headband and think to oneself, "Everything's coming up Jenna." That was not the case tonight.

After an unauthorized gerrymandering of her table section by some overzealous hostesses, which resulted in a far inferior workstation for the evening, things started to go awry. First she knocked the printer off the table at the server station and into the window, narrowly escaping shattering the glass but succeeding in drawing the attention of the entire restaurant with the ambiance-piercing crash. (*Sidenote: loud noises in a performance-based, staged work environment are awesome. The noise always seems to act like the needle across the record, stopping conversation and making every lemming turn toward the source.*) Clumsiness happens in the restaurant business, more often than not, when one is idle, and she was idle because an endless stream of patrons was being escorted to her section only to ask the hostess, "May we sit somewhere else?" Not because of Jenna herself, mind you, but the recent gerrymandering had given her a collection of the least desirable tables in the restaurant. The long and the short of it was that Jenna had no tables—and the night was only going to get longer.

In an effort to supply some sort of distraction, I brought her a sample of the sauce we would be using for the fish that evening. This particular delicacy is a lovely and well-balanced concoction of carrot, coconut, and curry. Upon one taste Jenna was clearly dismayed and exclaimed, "This is the grossest stuff I have ever tasted! And now it's taken over my mouth." If she ever got a table in her section that evening, Jenna would be selling no fish tonight because of the sauce it came with.

She excused herself for a pilgrimage to the guest restroom for some much-needed mouthwash relief. Much to her dismay, there was no more mouthwash.

I let her know that there was a small remaining portion in my office, and she quickly disappeared; she needed that taste out of her mouth and *quick!* The curry was seemingly staging a coup against all other ability to taste.

She returned glassy-eyed and laughing/crying. Jenna missed her mouth with the very last hurried shot of Listerine in the building and poured it down her shirt, spotting her uniform tie and vest. To everybody else she smelled like mouthwash, but her mouth was still under siege by curry and carrot.

Quickly another distraction was needed to alleviate dwelling on the moment, and the phone ringing provided the perfect simple task for Jenna to execute. I asked her to please answer the phone for me. She sauntered to the phone and picked it up. "Good evening and thank you for calling First Presbyterian Church"... silence... "I mean the Steak House." Oh, Jenna. Who would have ever guessed that the volunteer work you do at the church on the weekends would present itself as a blunder at your paying job? At this point I needed to dig deep to give her a reason to smile. A compliment that would make her feel good about her terrible, horrible, no-good, very bad day.

"At least you have a magnificent Technicolor headband today," I said, to which she honestly replied, "It's too tight and gives me a headache" —and I just happen to know that we are out of aspirin.

There's just no winning this one, and into all of our lives, a little Jenna must fall.

You're the Coolest Boss Ever

When I was striving to achieve solidarity with my workers as a "good manager," I was constantly evaluating my personal performance to make sure I was continually getting better at my profession or, if nothing else, making damn sure I wasn't moving backward. My initial mentor, Juliann, pulled me aside once and gave me the best advice I have ever received in management (even though it was the hardest pill to swallow at the time). She told me that under no certain terms, things were different now, and I could no longer "play" with the staff as peers.

Being as how I had risen to the ranks of management from
server at my first employment venue, my challenge became not
only to successfully lead the herd that I had once so freely
roamed with, but also to maintain the integrity of our new roles
in the form of respect for one another. This dance was imperative
while minimizing any animosity that most certainly would be
present when one rises in the ranks above others. In laymen's
terms this meant that it was no longer acceptable to be the
lampshade-on-the-head-wearing coworker at the after-hours
function for the evening or to crash on the couch of my server
friends because I had too much to drink after shift.

After this tutorial I became very aware of my new role as the
tie wearer, and made the decision to lead but always be
approachable—until one day, many moons later, I was hit with
the innocently delivered comment: "You're the coolest boss ever."
The simple line sent me into a tailspin. This topically harmless
compliment affected me the same way the word *quality* affected
the mighty Phaedrus in the book *Zen and the Art of Motorcycle
Maintenance*, spinning and spinning around inside his head being
pulled apart at imaginary seams. The sentence manifested itself
after an employee heard me telling another employee on the
phone to enjoy her family and extend her holiday another day
when the staffer called in around the holidays asking if she was
needed. "Don't worry about your shift, I can get it covered.
Family is what matters this time of year."

The truth was, we really weren't going to be all that busy and
I was probably going to call her off anyway, but it had a way of
painting me in a positive light of compassion and caring. Could
this quick comment be just that, quick and then possibly
forgotten? Not for the overanalytical mind that is the lump three
feet above my ass.

The passing employee heard my phone exchange and
without even slowing down uttered the daggerlike phrase,

"You're the coolest boss ever." This set me to hours of dissection. What does that mean? Is it a compliment? It sounded like one, but are bosses supposed to be cool?... and so on and so on.

"You're the coolest boss ever" is your typical example of a workplace fallacy. Examples of fallacies including, but not reserved for, double-edged sword, slippery slope, half-truths, straw men, and all the rest. While certainly not intended to be so by the server who attributed coolness to me, I couldn't help but use this innocent comment as a detailed snapshot of my managerial skills.

The first question I had to ask myself was, Do I think that *my* boss is cool? Why, yes, in a sense I do. I think he is a great, brilliant man who possesses the knowledge and patience to teach me how to bring my level of the game up a peg; but doesn't necessarily make him the "coolest."

Does that mean that ergo, I should not strive to be the "coolest" and should concentrate on being more like him? And what exactly is the intended definition of *coolest* in this particular instance? Is it the leather-jacket-donning, snubbing-the-women, cigarette-hanging-from-the-lip coolest that immediately comes to mind, or is it the hidden pushover, the softy I seemed to be based on the originating conversation that led me to this internal mental struggle?

While I love that my staffers seem to enjoy having me around and the feeling is certainly mutual, the title "coolest" could serve as an albatross around my neck (inserted fallacy accomplished)— and it becomes very hard to govern with a giant dead bird as a scarf. In my "adulthood" I have come to despise the symbolism of cool as the "don't give a shit" guy, and I certainly wouldn't want to be a pushover. I suppose most of me wishes she had said, "You're the most intelligent, witty, levelheaded, authoritative, and respected boss ever," because that is the kind of sentence that just rolls off the tongue freely, right?

So many questions arise from this small and topical complimentary sentence. After all, I want to be a positive energy kind of leader for those on my team, because you are only ever as good as those around you. And if coolness is a rung of achievement on the ladder to a successful career, then I emphatically embrace my new title "coolest," even if it implies that I have reached the final rung (which I haven't).

At the end of the day, I need to be a leader, and to lead is not always to be considered the coolest. Should I take the more mature approach that I have enough friends outside of work and don't necessarily need to consider shopping for my staff members' birthdays or let them ever see me in my pajamas? That could never be misconstrued as cool, but the reality is that I may just be overthinking this a bit. Instead I should have responded to said employee with "Thank you, I think you're pretty cool as well," and gone back to thinking about how important it is that the Athletics win tonight or that I hope the irritation on my ankle is a bug bite and not a rash. But then again, sentences and fallacies can be so much more entertaining with a scalpel and surgical mask and the pseudo-intelligence and patience to chop the hell out of them and see what you can turn them into.

Working with Staff: The Biz She Can Be Fickle

Working in the service industry allows for a deeper and more intense psychological analysis of one's inner workings and chemical makeup than perhaps that of a garbage collector or toll taker—not to demean any other form of gainful employment, mind you, but only to bring light to my own. And while it is true that most of the lessons one learns about personal thresholds come from the patrons, the lessons provided by fellow employees have no less significance and should always be observed and logged in an effort to better oneself as a leader.

By holding my breath and not physically ripping the head off the guy who wants to decant an earlier-that-year vintage of some local ten-dollar wine, I have learned the patience that others attempted to teach me in my earlier years, learned just to step back and count to ten, or repeat the time-tested mantra of "this too shall pass." Other lessons learned have come from watching the patterns and personal nuances of a staff. Between them, these teachers have elevated my acceptance of the human experience to the level of Jane Goodall and the gorillas she lived among. Let the record show that her and my studies are remarkably similar in regards to subject matter. Please also let the record reflect the use of the word *acceptance* as opposed to *understanding* in the previous sentence.

In a sick and twisted way, I suppose I never want to truly understand the things that service workers do, and may I remind myself that the frustrations that constantly bubble below the surface are merely the spices in the "all-day collard greens" that make the restaurant business so uniquely desirable. The major difference between a restaurant floor and a cubicle is that at the restaurant, no two days will ever be scripted the same way. Still, trends and traditions will predictably fall on specific days and times of the year, and never have curiosities been so revealed as during the coming and going of the holiday season in fine dining.

The holidays are a grand time, and long after one realizes that (spoiler alert) Santa is not real, the excitement and anticipatory facets remain. (*Sidenote: In my adult life I cling to the notion that the true three stages of life are (1) you believe in Santa; (2) you are Santa; (3) you look like Santa.*)

In fine dining and as adults we have all realized that the nail-biting and nervous shuffling associated with the holidays of our youth are no longer centered on whether we are going to get the Huffy from Sears that we wanted, but more on the adult desire for cold hard cash. The single most unarguable factor in the buzz around the holidays is that every brick-and-mortar building of commerce that houses a cash register will experience money being spent more freely. The holidays are an excellent lubricant for otherwise stiff wallets.

From a management perspective, this time of year is cultivated and planned for starting on February 15 and marketed endlessly until the final sprint starting October 31. The crucial dates we plan for include Christmas Eve, New Year's Eve, and Valentine's Day. This is our holiday season. Hence planning for the coming holidays begins the day after Valentine's Day, and the execution (or sprint portion of the marathon) happens the minute Halloween has arrived.

Halloween is not so much a revered holiday in the restaurant business because most good people are cultivating their families by putting their little ones in scary or silly outfits, marching them door to door, and netting them free candy—or, more important, being swing men who pass the candy out. Behind the scenes it is understood among staff and rarely hidden very deeply the disdain for people who eat in restaurants on All Hallows' Eve. This is simply due to the illusory belief that if these guests are at the restaurant eating, then somewhere in the world there is a dark porch with zero opportunity for candy acquisition by all the little clowns and cowgirls (but hopefully a 100 percent chance of a nice egging brought on by the misguided youth who are struggling with the fact that they are too old for free candy but still cleared to stay out late on a school night). (*Sidenote: most of these miscreants will end up working in the restaurant business later.*) But I digress. Planning for the approaching holidays starts somewhere during shift on October 31, when as managers we must look past any injustices that are possibly being committed by the solitary guest and use the downtime to look toward Christmas.

It is during this time of planning and execution that the staff dynamics of shock and awe strikes with an authoritative blow and leaves exhausted managers rubbing their heads in disbelief year after year. Every time we are convinced that next year will certainly be different; it must be! But it never is. Let us then paint a picture.

The time is just after the holidays have concluded, February 15ish, and we have, as a business, just spent the better part of a two months making money hand over fist. We have, as mangers, given every employee the adult Christmas gift of all of their desires in the form of extra shifts and every opportunity to pad their bankroll in preparation for the coming leaner months. I have always considered the holidays in F&B the "harvest season." The collection of the fruits of labor should have resulted in tree trunks stuffed with acorns for all of our squirrels, but apparently the squirrels have a selective short term memory and/or a lack imagination, for no sooner has the holiday season ended than the average staffer is astounded at the well running dry and in total disbelief at the injustices brought on by me personally as I trim shifts on the schedule.

Here is the message: You were told in no uncertain terms that these wonderful times were coming but would not last very long. How then could I possibly be responsible for the fact that it is now mid-February and you have nothing to show for your hard work short of a new tattoo, a terrific hangover, and a slew of posted Facebook pictures that you hardly remember taking or being a part of? In the rare instance that I have not become the target of enough malice, I must now suffer the slings and arrows of cutting the shifts that were once bountiful back to exactly what they were at the same time last year. For a month and a half the average server has gone from three to four shifts a week to the bountiful five to six with doubles. In addition, most of these shifts involved an endless round of banquets and holiday parties, where throngs of seasonal drinkers had an excuse to get drunk in the middle of the day with dozens of coworkers all on the company tab, and the ever-present "auto-gratuity" was in full effect.

Did the average staffer for one minute believe that this phenomenon was less about the time of year, and more about the personal celebration. That the servers in question had really proved themselves to be model employees and were only just now reaping their just reward? Why, yes, that seems to be the consensus. Then at the precise moment that the fields become semi-barren again, they line up outside the office door and politely ask why they are being punished. Did they do something wrong? How can they maintain the shifts that they had last month?

This is not a passive-aggressive employee evaluation, and I am not sending a management message masked in the cutting of shifts. The fact remains that fewer people are coming into the restaurant right now to spend buckets of money because it is March and there is no reason for them to be here. Remember last year? Same thing happened just like this and at exactly the same time of year.

I stop short of telling each person to "grow up," but more often than not, this is exactly what needs to happen. There needs to be foresight, execution, and planning to cultivate success, and any one factor without the other results in immediate failure. Know that the holidays are approaching and remember what this time was like the year prior. Work your butt off tirelessly at the apex of the season and collect any and all shifts and money that you can while the picking is good. There will be time to rest later. And, most important, save! Put the funds that you are collecting to use later, not by opening a tab at the pub for you and fifteen of your closest friends. Just like the guests at the restaurant, those magic friends of yours won't be there in March either.

As a manager, I accept my role in the debacle as well, as I am not without responsibility in this case. We go out of our way to hire presentable twenty-somethings for the enjoyment of the guests and then abhor them for acting young. This particular rant is for the staffer who has been there long enough to recognize patterns in the operation, regardless of age. If you are old enough to be gainfully employed, then you should be old enough to act like it. On any given day and at any given time of the year, I consider myself beyond lucky to work with the unique individuals that I get to work with on a daily basis (the movie *Empire Records* has the manager lovingly refer to his staff as all of his "tattooed gum-chewing freaks"), and love—*love!*— the cultivation of relationships with the people around me. But there are just some times in any family structure when I would just as soon give them all collectively a Viking funeral... even if they aren't all quite dead yet. (*Sidenote: a Viking funeral consists of setting the bodies adrift on a raft covered in flammable materials, and then shooting flaming arrows at said raft from the shore until the whole contraption is set ablaze on the water.*)

This just happens to be a very fitting analogy for the level of animosity I feel toward the aforementioned levels of stupidity.

Scheduling

Everywhere I have worked, it has been my not-so-rare but very dubious honor to be the person responsible for scheduling the employees who worked the floor. Thank goodness for executive chefs, if for no other reason than that they take care of scheduling the back of the house (cooks, dishwashers, chefs, and so on) for people like me, singlehandedly wiping 50 percent of my ulcer-causing job duties off the map. Ask anybody who has held the illustrious job of F&B manager what the bane of their existence is, and they should all chime in, in unison, "schedules." The one guy who says "the hours worked" is already too jaded to continue fruitfully in their role, and mark my words, that manager will be collecting tolls in a booth somewhere before the year is over.

For a long time I have been constructing the schedule one week at a time (just writing that has implanted the brilliant idea of creating a support group for those of us lucky enough to endeavor "one week at a time") or—in the rare case of where I was last employed—three weeks at a time. In my own personal mental schedule, Thursdays are my scheduling days, and this area of management is one of only two days that I have marked and set aside for a specific tasks all week, the other being Wednesday, our manager meeting day. Unlike Wednesdays, though, I fear and loathe Thursdays because there is no positive payoff. Not ever!

After the completion of any task, be it at the restaurant or in one's personal life, there is always the possibility that you will have learned a valuable life lesson that you can grow from, or possibly even net a positive outcome that you had not foreseen and are pleasantly delighted to discover. This alone is what has members of the human race pushing themselves into arenas foreign to them and testing the boundaries of perseverance— sort of a "let's open the hood and tinker a bit, then take her on the track and see what she is made of." But not scheduling. The only joy I get when I complete a schedule is that the task has been completed and will not be reattempted in its entirety for the next seven days. That is not to say that I won't be drawn back to the computer numerous times over the next few days to correct the mistakes (in staff members' eyes) that I have made, which will be pointed out to me with relish as every individual employee enters the building at staggered entry times over the next few days and lays eyes on the abomination of my handiwork posted in the service station.

Every time I complete the initial feat of the weekly schedule, I always say out loud, to nobody in particular, "Okay—let's go trolling for complaints!" because that is exactly what I am doing. The hope is not that I may have nailed it this time; the hope is simply that I don't get more than a dozen angry staffers. It is amusing to see the faces of people trudging to the wall in the server station and peering at the schedule for the approaching week. The life drains out of them and their formerly content demeanor is replaced with outrage at my seemingly evil ways. Gasping for breath at my blatant misunderstanding of the injustices they are suffering, they reach my position and rattle off spitting rebuttals—things like "You know that I am having a mole removed that day," "You said I could have that day off to participate in the soapbox derby," "I never work Wednesdays; what the hell?" "Man, I have a tee time on Tuesday," or my favorite, "That day is just not going to work out for me."

Before any reader may decide I am lacking in compassion, it should be absolutely understood that I really don't make many changes at all. For the most part, the schedule set forth is the same as it has been for months, and I have the computer program to prove it, but the gnat-like memory of the average server/busser leads them to believe that every week is constructed anew and based on my sheer desire to see everyone suffer.

The process is as follows: I have and do collect daily "request off" sheets from all employees and file them in one single folder that I call my schedule bible. Never mind the small details like I have a preset and printed form for these requests available at every workstation throughout the restaurant, I still gather more requests scribbled on bar napkins than not and I have gotten to be okay with that; as long as they fit in the bible, I'm good. First things first, I weed out and process all requests for the week I am dealing with and file the rest for later. I respectfully mark an "RO" on any dates in question next to a server's name on the actual schedule, meaning "requested off."

Let me stop myself right there. I don't have to do any of this, as the very title of the form says "request." At most points in life this term is used so that with little or no thought, said request can be denied; but I am so over-the-moon happy that most people have had the wherewithal to think about their future scheduling conflicts more than seven days in advance that I have yet to deny a request off form. Second, I look at the calendar of upcoming events at the restaurant and mark special events in HUGE BOLD LETTERS at the bottom of the daily column, allowing any and all servers who may be getting an unusual schedule a brief description of the reason for it—e.g., "SMITH BANQUET, 150 PEOPLE."

"Yes, I realize that you don't usually work on Wednesdays, but you see here, I have a banquet for 150 people that night and it will require a few extra bodies." It should also be noted here that there are only two times a server or busser speaks about the schedule, and they are day and night; and there are only two things they talk about, and they are the injustice of being scheduled on a day they don't usually come in or the equally popular complaint about not having enough shifts. There is no time in between. It is seriously that frequent and that bipolar. Sprinkle my task with the daunting floating "on-call" shifts that rotate every Monday, Tuesday, Wednesday, and Thursday and I have just chummed the waters for my complaint sharks to swim into with a flurry.

I have endured a lot of personal challenges while managing restaurants and have slowly perfected the art of dismantling bomb-like scenarios tableside. And I most certainly am required to handle all situations, no matter how detrimental to my personal state, with an expression of calm and comfort; but the sole bane of my existence is scheduling employees. It is truly where managers earn their money, and not nearly enough of it.

CHAPTER 7

Guests

Here is where we get to the nuts and bolts of the whole operation of food and beverage service—the carefully orchestrated dance between the logical and the pure insanity that is not only dealt with in the many forms it arrives in but is sickly sought after. The very fodder for the original inspiration behind this book, my blog, so appropriately named "Careful, This Could Get Messy."

In a perfect world, restaurants would operate in a utopian manner in which every single guest would come into the building with a hunger that they were excited to conquer and leave with the feeling of euphoria that comes with a wonderful meal and so much more. Comments from near and far could be barely heard by server spies as the people at the table mutter under their collective breaths about how professional the young lady helping them has been, and have you ever tasted a fish so succulent in all of your life? Then upon seeing the server just out of eye's range someone at the table calls her over to bless her with a subtle (not too over-the-top) verbal compliment while pulling more than the suggested 18 percent cash tip from a wallet so as to silently suggest, "Don't worry, the verbal compliment has a paper accompaniment." Then when leaving the building with one hand placed lovingly on their full gullets, these guests ask the hostess to see the manager; when he or she arrives, they promptly launch into a well-woven tapestry of praise for the evening's experience and recognition of the endless hard work that must have been done by said manager (paper accompaniment not necessary).

But alas, while this does happen exactly as scripted on a not-so-regular basis, the situation is more often dictated by individuals who feel empowered by having selected this specific restaurant to spend their hard-earned money, and try as you might, their expectations have not been met, simply because they were jaded when they arrived and they will be jaded when they leave. This is the "this better be good" mentality, and it seems to be the Siamese twin of the service industry.

Do not misinterpret my devotion and desire for guests to have an experience they were not expecting on the positive side. That is precisely the outcome that we train tirelessly for and demand from our staff. Any person getting ready for a night out should know firsthand that in the hours before and behind the scenes of any nicer place the players are getting ready for your arrival by polishing silverware and stemware in eager anticipation of knocking your socks off with the quality and kindness you deserve. Resilient is the staffer who on a day-to-day basis washes the semantic sludge slung by any jerk the night before by properly sponge-bathing at the tavern late into the night previous, so that now said jerk is nothing more than another footnote on the pile of stories in the archives. "That guy" from table 62 last night is no more remembered than the chicken wings that accompanied the fourth pitcher of beer at Jack's Pub and Grub at 1:00 A.M., and as jaded as any one person has a right to be, usually the staff shows up mentally clean, with a canvas ready to receive this night's paints... *usually.*

Make no mistake that one single ass in a sea of otherwise successful tables can (and does) derail a server during a shift, and my greatest hope in sitting down to write this book lies in the idea that I may provide some sort of manual for how to make your and the staff's experience a positive one.

"That Guy"

As management, we appreciate your presence in the restaurant with every fiber in our being, and not only will we do anything on the spot that will help facilitate the belly-rubbing, ooh-and-ahhing, complimenting-through-grinning-lips experience that you so much deserve, we have also gone two steps further in training the people around us how to deliver these special moments. In short, we are professionals; and while we may look like God's throw-backs, confuse the layperson with speculations about just exactly what in life would transpire to have a sixty-year-old man and a twenty-year-old young woman dressed in the same uniform and unfolding a napkin across your lap, rest assured that as individuals we are very good at what we do.

The fact remains that the guest is the rookie. People can eat out in restaurants all their lives and not "get it." This becomes one of the key lessons that must be taught, and hopefully taught early enough so that when diners come into any establishment to eat they are not only coming to feed the hunger that strikes on average three times a day, but to carefully hone their skills at being courteous diners. (*Sidenote: one of my favorite quotes by Luciano Pavarotti and William Wright is, "One of the very nicest things about life is the way that we must stop whatever it is we are doing and devote our attention to eating."*)

Fortunately enough, this is a dog that can be taught new tricks, and just because you saw your father smack the ass of his waitress on a regular basis when you were growing up or your mom constantly sent back food doesn't mean that you are doomed to a lifetime of being "that guy." (*Sidenote: in the business we commonly refer to jerks, assholes, negative dicks, bad tippers, and*

all their tribe as "that guy." It is an all-encompassing term that is
understood among service people. The last thing you ever want to be is
"that guy," whether you are a man or a woman, as "that guy" has no
gender specificity.)

However, the fact is not wasted on most of us that the
opportunity never presents itself for us to shed the light of
practical knowledge on the diner so as to achieve an enlightened
state. Whenever a situation presents itself where somebody is
acting inappropriately, to launch into any type of tutorial would
only be perceived as an insult by the person who is acting out.
And remember that everything in this business is fast-paced. We
are not serving food in a Learning Annex at an all-day F&B
exposition equipped with overhead transparencies of pie charts.
We are instead having situations flung at us with the velocity of
a spoonful of mashed potatoes in a food fight, and acting
impulsively in reaction. There is little room in this scenario for
stepping back, catching one's breath, and taking a healthy look
at the situation in order to draw a conclusion that will be
appreciated by everybody. Things of a negative nature more
commonly result in a "Fuck you!" "Oh, yeah, well fuck you!"
ending, and nobody wins. My sheer desire here is to take the
Learning Annex approach and give some solid advice to the
people who really need to hear it—and even those who don't.

Let us all take a step back, count to ten, and turn to page
blank in our unwritten textbooks, where we will find actual
scenarios that have helped sculpt opinions on how it should be
done by those very people who receive their money from where
you spend it. This is by no means directed at you (yeah, right),
it is more directed at "that guy," the one that you as a patron
have seen berating the twenty-year-old server to the brink of
tears or making the sixty-year-old man feel terrible about the
past life choices that led him to be here wearing a vest and taking
your order—but then again, as stated much earlier, I have a
tendency to cater to the people who wouldn't even know it was

them if I called them by name. Chances are, however, that you will know if you are guilty of any of the F&B no-nos we are about to study, and if nothing else your awareness can prevent their happening in the future. After all, we are all, as staff and patron, just looking for that over-the-rainbow experience that has you smiling and patting people like me on the back as you walk out of the restaurant murmuring to nobody in particular, "Nice meal, nice job!"

Hot Tea and the Verbal Tip

It doesn't escape my notice that on the surface, this seems like an oddly paired duo, and they may sound to you more like a pair of crime-fighting superheroes. But make no mistake about it: these are two constant sources of bile-building animosity in the restaurant business. These topics of many a fury-laden tirade can be heard ad nauseam around what is commonly referred to as "the water cooler" in any office setting, but is known as the "service/server station" in the restaurant biz.

The service station is a sacred area where employees are forced to gather, away from the guests but with their respected peers, to refill sodas, collect bread and butter, obtain a clean knife to replace the one that fell on the floor (quite possibly the same one wiped off with a damp cloth), retrieve water and coffee pitchers, or snatch up lemon, sugars, and so on. But the most valuable aspect of the service station is the opportunity it provides for momentarily dropping off any semantic blockage that may be weighing the server down at any particular moment. This is done with a colorfully woven tapestry of verbiage that would make any sailor blush. The ironic aspect of the service station is that it lies in close proximity to the diners themselves so as to ensure faster service, but none the wiser is the patron about what is being said a mere two inches of sheetrock away.

More often than not, and because of the fact that these are not your typical counseling sessions or even deep, meaningful conversations but rather a pipe-cleaning tirade lasting only seconds, the two topics most often centered on are hot tea and the verbal tip. These are items that any server understands on more than a rudimentary level, and no explanation is needed to gain a colleague's sympathy.

Here is just a small sample of what may be heard as the servers dash from gathering point to gathering point in the spacious ten-by-ten-foot room while simultaneously mopping their brows to get ready to go back out on the floor: "Table 62 just gave me the verbal tip, and then ordered three fuckin' hot teas!"

Let's break it down.

The "verbal tip" is the kiss of death for any server, anywhere on the globe.

The meal is almost done, and the server is in "go" mode, making sure that the final minutes before you enter the gratuity on the check are amazingly memorable in the most positive way, despite the fact that your steak was undercooked, or your favorite table wasn't available. That is all ancient history. We need to make sure that when it comes time to scribble in the tip, only smiles abound at the table. Then it happens—the patron touches the server's arm and says, "You were a fantastic server, thank you so much."

Aaauuugh! The server never even saw it coming. This is the verbal tip. As soon as the bill is laid down, and the verbal tip applied, the actual tip is scratched in... 10 percent (or worse). Most verbal tippers actually think that the compliment translates to cash!

The server dreams of saying, "Thank you so much for the kind words, I'll just put them here in my self-addressed stamped envelope and mail them to my landlord. I'm sure he'll think that's more than adequate for this month's rent."... *Don't do it!*

Let your monetary tip be the compliment or even, in the best of scenarios, give both. It is always nice to hear how good one is at one's job, but equate that to something I can break into ones and roll around in on my bed before giving it all to the electric company so that the lights can stay on another day.

Second thing—hot tea. This can most commonly be referred to as "the straw that broke the camel's back," "the nail in the coffin," or any other number of colorful expressions denoting a cause for derailment. Yes, it's true, most restaurants offer an assortment of teas because if we didn't the judgment would hurt more than the task. In addition, as a manager, once the product is ordered and put into circulation, the tea is no longer my concern and falls squarely on the shoulders of the service staff; but as one may have gathered by now, my voice is for the little guys and how to make life just a little more tolerable in their profession. The rule of thumb here is simple: unless you are dining at a Chinese food establishment or are a hundred years old and medically cleared to drink only one beverage, hot tea is the worst item you can order, and it will evoke eye rolls and shit talk around our water cooler.

The simple fact of the matter is that hot tea takes seven steps to complete for just one order. *Seven steps!* I don't even take that many steps to get dressed in the morning. Think about that for a moment while I break it down: cup and saucer (I'm even counting this as one, not two), hot water pot, sugar, cream, spoon, and lemon, all balanced precariously atop a bulky non-server-friendly tea box, and all this for a staggering two bucks. Add to the fact that because of all of these steps, the busboy will magically disappear and be nowhere to be found merely from overhearing the order. All this just boils down to... you're screwed. (*Sidenote: you will never find any people who have ever worked in F&B fine dining order tea for themselves when dining out... ever; and if they do, then they are the very people I referred to earlier as those who just don't get it.*) Nothing can send the tempo of a well-orchestrated dance off-kilter in a busy section faster than somebody who chooses hot tea over coffee.

Let's recap. Hot tea in Chinese restaurant... good, they plan for it and it is most certainly part of the overall experience! Hot tea in any other restaurant... c'mon, man, what's wrong with coffee? My busboy will get *that*!

And we don't really care if we do remind you of your son or daughter who is off at school making something better of themselves, or that you haven't been this pampered since your honeymoon twenty-five years ago, the compliment is completely wasted if you don't translate it into cash. Always keep in mind that the server is tipping a percent of total *sales* to the support staff (busser, runner, bartender, sommelier, and the rest) not a percentage of tips—a fact that is commonly misunderstood—so a 9 percent tip on a two-hundred-dollar bill is going to send the server paying out of pocket... it's a loss. It doesn't have to be this way.

Consider yourselves learned.

Advanced Placement: Table for One

Tear them down only to build them back up again. That is the theme of this screed I'm sharing with you. So far my words could be deemed harsh, and were this a real class at the Learning Annex I might suggest that we break here for lunch, as I am quite certain that some may need to go get a Kleenex or punch a wall, having recently realized either that you have violated said unwritten rules at one time or another on a regular basis or that you have come to the conclusion that I am a pompous, self-righteous windbag.

Either way, I will launch into my next lesson as soon as the tears and anger have retreated a bit, for what follows is what I would consider to be the F&B insider's solid gold, the real meat and potatoes of positive advice that will leave any potential patron licking his chops for more. This then is a tutorial on how and where to dine alone in a restaurant while maximizing your solo experience.

When I lived in downtown Oakland, I would treat myself to a lavish dinner for one at least once a week. No, I was not in particular need of company; I was not a lonely person. I truly consider the art of being comfortable alone pursuing any number of activities that one would do with other people a soul-feeding necessity, and one not explored nearly enough by people who worry too much about what other people must think.

First of all, if you are dining alone, pick a place with a bar and make sure you sit there and there only. Nobody wants to be, or look at, the creepy person on a dining room floor peering over the risotto at all the other happy couples or four-tops. This is precisely the time when any responsible person should be aware of and care what others may think because you have just gone out of your way to embody a stigma. You may as well get the rest of your food packed up to go and get into your van with no windows and head back to your bed under the bridge behind the elementary school. Bottom line is, either you're a food critic or this looks creepy.

Now—not just any seat at the bar will do. Solo diners need to position themselves as close as possible to (preferably next to) the service bar.

This area is usually marked by tall brass handles, the obligatory bar mat, and the ever-present cocktail condiment caddy of olives, onions, cherries, limes, and twists. It is where all the servers will go to retrieve any beverages ordered on the dining room floor that need to be prepared by the bartender. The service bar is yet another "water cooler" of the restaurant office, like that of the service station, but this one includes the mighty bartender, who is sure to have a couple of zingers to add to any banter and who rarely gets to retreat to the real service station to vent with his/her colleagues. (*Sidenote: "water coolers" can be defined as places where the manic pace of service is forced to stop in the name of commerce—drinks must get made and you must wait, or napkins must be folded and you must stop.*) The brilliant part about when the quick-witted, forked-tongued staff gets a chance to stop for a moment is that laughter and guffaws abound in rapid-fire procession.

Before you sit at your position near or at the service bar it is crucial that you be armed with props that allow you to commingle with the staff as one of their own, without being noticed. Like any wild animals being observed in their natural environment, foodies will silence themselves immediately and pull up shop if the foreigner (you) shows the slightest interest. So it becomes crucial that you look like you're not really listening at all. Do not assume the establishment will have a television for you to fake-watch. Come prepared with a magazine or book, and be prepared to not read a word. Here is where your ears are your asset, not your eyes.

If you're frequenting a particular establishment for a while, take the time to learn table numbers. A study guide can be obtained by stopping by the hostess stand and asking one of the tweenies (young hostess) for a copy of the floor plan to take home. If she is suspicious about your request (which she won't be because OMG she is totally waiting for the tattooed guy to text and tell her if they are going to Brittany's kegger) then tell her it is so you have a reference point for your favorite places to sit when you make your reservations. This floor map will provide a visual aid for the endless tidbits of industry gossip you are about to devour.

Let the Games Begin!

Two servers are patiently waiting for their gin-and-tonics to be made while you are posted up like a *National Geographic* photographer behind your camouflage copy of the *Wall Street Journal*.

Server 1: "Did you see the rack on the girl on table 22? I would wear that like a hat."

Server 2: "I got a biggun on table 57. She ordered a twenty-four-ounce bone-in rib-eye, extra peppercorn sauce, side of mac and cheese, creamed spinach, baked potato and a *diet* coke. Who the hell is she kidding with *diet*?"

Server 1: "How much do you think the guy with the comb-over on 62 is paying for his date with that escort?"

Enter bartender with made drinks: "Dude on seat 12 has the worst breath ever—seriously smells like he's been eating shit sandwiches and the fucker just ordered extra garlic on his calamari. Gonna be a long night."

Server 1: "Did you hear that Alex and Chris hooked up last night?"

Server 2: "She's the town bike, man—everybody's had a ride."

Exit servers bar left armed with their cocktails ready to serve.

Devilishly you smile, not just because you went unnoticed and could make out every word, and not just because you had the wherewithal to memorize table numbers and can get a visual on the people the staff are talking about the next time you visit the bathroom and get a glance at the floor, but you realize this whole scenario will repeat itself endlessly throughout the night and you haven't even been served your salad.

Seriously, I should bill you for this information.

Should I Stay or Should I Go?

The following is fodder for many a heated debate between staffers and guests. This is the breakdown of the true importance and hidden definition of the posted "hours of operation." Go figure that I lean toward the side of the staffer and often have a jaded opinion of personal interpretations of how closely somebody should tread to the opening and closing times of a restaurant. That's so unlike me so far... right?

The testing of said waters will not make or break an evening on the surface—that is to say, you as the guest will not be subjected to endless distress while you try diligently to choke down your meal if only to end the glares from a perturbed staff as closing time approaches. However; that is not to say that you aren't the subject matter of many eye-rolls and under-the-breath mutterings of the designated closer for the evening. Because it behooves the staff to put on their happy faces when faced with the recurring issue of the late-night diner, my firm belief is that people should know exactly what the etiquette is so that they may ensure the full positive experience that is dining out.

First and foremost, any potentially decent person can decipher right off the bat the difference between a restaurant and any other retail store with posted hours. Using a public announcement would be pretty silly in the context of dining out. Could you imagine a bartender grabbing a microphone and stating to all people in the store, "We will be closing in fifteen minutes. Please gather your final scraps of food and make your way to the front of the building for purchase"? (Pause here for fond fantasy gazing at the perfect world that would allow for such an event; but alas, it is just that—a fantasy.) In reality, everything that takes place in a restaurant takes time, and the examples here use a twenty-minute general formula that represents approximately the time necessary for preparation and execution. Beware—there is some light math in the following lesson.

Scenario One

It is Tuesday night and you know that your favorite restaurant closes the kitchen at 9:00 P.M. You're in your La-Z-Boy and sweatpants watching *Dancing with the Stars* as you look up at the clock on the wall and see that it reads 8:30.

You quickly do the math internally because you're so smart you don't need a calculator. 8:30 + 10-minute commute + 12-

minute order time = 8:52 pm. *Yes*—under 9:00! You then proceed to shout to your better half in the back room, "Fetch me my heels and fanny pack, Hon, were goin' out!"

Hold on there, Pythagoras! Your internal calculator may be working like gangbusters; however, your math does not include the implied restaurant formula of immediately adding on twenty minutes to said starting time. Let us put you back into your La-Z-Boy to redo the math. If the clock on the wall reads 8:30 when your mighty belly rumbles for the first time of the night, then this means it is really 8:50 when you have begun to internally compartmentalize your "goin' out" checklist.

The implied formula exists simply because the whole dining experience takes time. In one second you have made a decision that will involve travel, reading, choosing, preparations, serving, consuming, picking, and finally paying. The unsung victims of this crime against time are the staffers.

Well outside the imagination of most guests in a restaurant are the images of what a person is like or does when the tie and apron come off. I imagine that most guests truly believe that at the end of a shift, I toggle the switch on the back of the staff members' necks and place them lovingly in the storage locker until their next shift. However, these people who work feverishly to please, actually have places to go and people to see, and not unlike anybody else living for quitting time, they relish the opportunity to make plans after their day is over. (*Sidenote: it is no secret that foodies practice a higher rate of social drinking and wasting of nightly funds after nearly every shift and can more often than not be found right next door with the tie just loosely slipped, not removed, imbibing with like species from different herds all over the area. But seldom recognized is the ever-present professional who just spent six hours slaving over a hot stove to get your medium-rare just right times a hundred patrons, and who really has to get home because his eight-year-old needs help with her math and his newborn has a gnarly head cold. Those exist as well.*)

Bottom line here is that you should enjoy your Mickey Mouse slippers a while longer, get involved in another dose of Tom Bergeron's witty banter on *AFV*, and perhaps fetch yourself a Cup Noodles instead of the previously sought heels and fanny pack. You should stay in.

Scenario Two

You arrive at the bar at 8:30 already dressed and ready for the evening.

You have already done the math and clothing preparations, all the while knowing that the kitchen closes at 9:00 P.M., but your thought process is that you have thirty minutes to spare. Again, let's go to the board. *8:30 + 20 minutes from formula = 8:50.* This is indeed enough time for you to glance at a menu, make a snap decision, and order fast, but instead you nurse your delicious house wine and flirt with the girl you just met and somehow convinced to let you buy her dinner in the hopes that she will be "the one." The very girl who will eventually spend all your money and leave you in the gutter with poop pants and an alcohol problem, and just that quickly the clock reads 8:57.

"We are ready to go to our table now," you mutter because you just can't wait to pick the cheapest thing on the menu that will take the allotted twenty minutes to cook, only to send it back and have it cooked again, so you can lose yourself in the eyes of the girl you're sure will produce a beautiful family that your mother will be proud of, and she can return the gaze into the eyes of her free meal ticket.

No, no, no, Chief! Wrong move—nobody wants to watch you slip into oblivion with your fantasy date when, as good family people, they know that there is an angry spouse waiting for them to get home to help with the kid or, if they're single, a frothy cocktail waiting for them at the local watering hole that stays open way past 9:00 on Tuesday. You know the place. It is right next door and the posted hours say "open until 11 daily." This is place you should have gone to from the get-go.

Bottom line is—you should go.

Scenario Three

You made an 8:30 reservation and arrived on time. You and your partner are really enjoying being out of the house, so much so that you told your server how happy you were for the midweek break as soon as you sat. The clock reads 8:45 and you apologize for taking so much time and ask for suggestions. In this scenario, communication reigns supreme. You, my friend, have just bought yourself as much time as you need, well past the posted time of 9:00 P.M., and the twenty-minute formula does not apply to you, as long as you get your order in before 8:50ish.

Why is this person different? Let us dissect the scene.

First, they made a reservation, and that is more than respected by staff. We knew that this person was coming and knew four hours in advance that we might be a little later than normal that evening. Plenty of time to call whoever might be affected by timing issues in order to alter plans.

Second, they were on time and, while ordering later than normal, have made verbal recognition of the reality that he understands the time issue and apologizes for any inconvenience.

Finally, this person is genuinely having a good time, and all the server has to do is ensure that it continues in order to reap the benefit monetarily. This is well worth staying later.

Bottom line: you can stay.

The argument has been offered that perhaps restaurants should have not only a "closing time" but also a "last seating time" that allows for the twenty-minute formula to take effect. The problem is that on the surface, the two closing times would leave people confused, and managers like me would spend more countless hours explaining the two times than implementing them, only to have Rico Suave still come in ten minutes after last seating with a party of six.

The simple advice to any person who absolutely must come in ten minutes before service ends and stay for two hours is that before you exit the building, take a short walk around the restaurant and hand hundred-dollar bills to everyone on the kitchen staff, the manager, the bartender, and the busboy—all of whom you have forced to make late phone calls to the people they promised they would be "there" by 9:30 and it is now midnight.

You would have to pay a prostitute for screwing her; why should we be any different?

I'm Going to Make His Head Explode... Watch!

Into everybody's restaurant a little "that guy" must fall.

I had a gentleman who was a regular at the steak house where I worked, and the exact reason that this man chose this place to frequent is still beyond my comprehension. Many an analytical conversation was sparked at slow times in the restaurant among any number of staffers on this mysterious subject. Suffice it to say perhaps that no matter what a horse's ass you are, you still need people to recognize you.

This man and his abiding temper served as a unifier among front-of-house and back-of-house employees, as each and every one of us had at one time or another been affected by this garbage-can-dwelling, matted-green-fur grouch and his Asian mail-order bride with an equally (I'm sure learned) sweet disposition. Usually on any given visit I was able to steer clear of this man and his "little black raincloud" approach to life; I would simply bow my head in understanding to the server, busser, bartender, and line cook who would be receiving this man's nightly tirade. But one day I was summoned and quite simply, I was not in the mood.

The server approached me and said that we inadvertently undercooked table 301's wife's steak. A quick glance at who we were dealing with revealed four diners—Mr. Sunshine, his dragon wife, and two guests whom I had never seen. While this "undercooked steak" was not an isolated occurrence by any stretch of the imagination, the last part of the request was. This prince among men was *demanding* a free glass of wine for his "put-off wife" as a form of payment for inconvenience. I quickly retreated to the nearest p.o.s. (point of sale computer) to pull up his tab and see just what I was dealing with. Wouldn't you just know it, she was having the twenty-five-dollar glass of Nickel and Nickel.

Being the "glass half full" type that I am, I did not trust that any person, even Señor Blood Pressure, could be so blindly angry about medium-rare instead of medium that he would demand a twenty-five-dollar glass of wine, so I proceeded to investigate.

"Good evening, Sir, nice to see you again. I understand that we undercooked your wife's steak."

"Where the hell is my free wine?" (What ever happened to "Hello"?)

Wow—this guy was for real. I was like a deer in headlights, but then I remembered: I had had a really bad month. A month chock-full of repression and emotion. A month of earth-shaking internal questions like should I work, or should I stay home. The bottom line for me at that moment was "Bring it on, asshole, I have been waiting for you for a month!" and somewhere in the far distance the sound of "Eye of the Tiger" could be heard while an imaginary Mickey was telling me to "eat nails and crap thunder!"

What I needed was one properly placed comment on exactly how this process was going to go, delivered with just the right amount of powdered-sugar kindness that as a manager I had been trained to deliver, would set the tone for the coming battle royal. My advantage was simply that I knew it was coming, but El Neck Vein didn't.

"We are working right now to correct our mistake in the kitchen, and I would be happy to bring your wife a nice glass of wine while she waits the [unthinkable] four minutes that this will take. However, I will be bringing her a glass of the Souverain [at an eight-dollar price]."

Like a short fuse on a powder keg, the high-strung man erupted. "Blah blah blah, save a few bucks on me will you, blah blah, arg arg, leave my table, arg arg." He was so spitting mad that he was having a hard time forming sentences, and he actually brushed my presence away with the back of his hand in a sweeping motion. Inside I was beaming sunshine at having reduced him to a babbling idiot, and as a bonus that I never saw coming, his guests looked mortified by their host's actions and are looking at me like POWs as if silently asking, "Isn't there anything you can do to get us out of here?" I threw them a wink to acknowledge their pain and apologize for their choice of dinner companion.

Twenty-five-dollar glass of Reserve Chardonnay or eight-dollar glass of house white really means nothing in the grander scheme of things, and the proper procedure for me would have been to swallow pride once again and appease this man while we admitted that we were the cause of this debacle in the first place. Another defining point that this man was completely unaware of was that I was never going to bring him a glass of our house wine anyway and in the end, I left and returned with his wife's twenty-five-dollar glass of Nickel and Nickel, as I intended to do from the start. However, I got the sick satisfaction of watching this man try to eat a steak through clenched teeth with bulging neck veins, while he felt me smiling at him the remainder of the evening, silently communicating to him my small victory and envisioning this scenario playing out again someday—perhaps here or perhaps at another eatery, but in time resulting in a major coronary because this man was wound too tightly and any wrenching on his spool of wire could cause him to snap at any minute. And this is how managers tip themselves.

After the dust settled, and around the water cooler, we determined that this was probably a person who yells and screams all day long to get what he wants at work and has been doing it for so long that he is physically unable to turn it off. The world has enough misery; what's the use of a perpetuator?

The bottom line is that restaurants mess up, and when we do, we will gladly make it right, whatever the problem. The secret is that you can have anything you want in the building for free, the more understanding, levelheaded, and calm you are. We respond much more openly to "I'm sorry, but I'm just not happy with my food" than to "Ra Ra cooked wrong, ugh ugh free shit now, blah blah arg arg I'm a dick" approach.

Gestures

In most instances, from roadside diners to semi-fine dining, the manager is required to wear all hats at the restaurant. In some corporate places this is part of the manager's training. We spend three months as a host, three months as line cook, three months as a bartender, and three months as a runner/expediter and are constantly honing our skills as bussers as well as picking up tables to serve when called upon. This allows the salaried manager to step in on slower occasions and save payroll by sending key hourly employees home for the evening. It can be a humbling experience and serves to keep us connected to the staff and the guests on a service level.

Just recently I was playing my usual Wednesday night runner/expo role of receiving the food from the window, wiping the edges of the plates, and checking the corresponding ticket one more time for table numbers and seat positions before heading out with the bounty. I set a beautiful halibut in front of an elderly gentleman while verbally describing the dish as such—i.e., "And a beautiful halibut for the gentleman." No sooner had I turned on my heel to retreat back to the window and expo the next ticket than I heard the deafening sound of fingers snapping from behind me.

Snapping! This sound supersedes all other sounds in the restaurant when it happens at the inappropriate time, and believe you me, there is no appropriate time. As I turned to see the source of this insult, the elderly man stated, "I need lemons." Sure, there was no "please" or "excuse me" from him, but I didn't expect such pleasantries based on the fact that he had snapped his way past them.

Here's the deal. Inevitably and invariably, you will need to get the attention of the service staff at some point, and usually "on the fly" or quickly, but not unlike most procedures in the dining experience there are really right ways and really wrong ways to do this. The best plan of action is to prepare for such events directly upon being greeted by your server. Most servers should greet the table by introducing themselves, if they are not already wearing a name tag; therefore as a guest you should take the time to listen or read this person's name and commit it to memory. Their parents gave it to them so that people could use it and immediately set them apart from the people around them.

On the off chance that the server did not introduce him or herself, and you are lucky enough to be dining at an establishment that does not use name tags, ask for the person's name, and even follow it up with a table introduction. Not only is there nothing wrong with getting to know the people who will be a part of your "today" story, but why shouldn't you be on a first-name basis with a person that who is handling your food and beverage, and dictating the outcome of your desire for an entertaining night out? After monikers have been established (again at the beginning of your meal), you should now feel safe to use this information (sparingly) at a moment's notice should you be left wanting for something during the duration of the meal. Furthermore, you can know that by using said moniker you are not instantly pushing the self-destruct button on service.

Quite often it is understood that the hustle and bustle of getting seated, receiving menus, and getting introduced to your server, all while anticipating a well-deserved night out, may result in the nonretention of names. There is still a right way and a wrong way to achieve the desired attention. Never... never, *never* is it all right to snap, whistle, yell, grab, make up a name on the spot, say "hey," or raise your arm to get the attention you need from any employee in the building. The only two things that are setting you apart from a two-year-old needing attention in this illustrative list are crying and pooping yourself, and if you feel the need to do any of the above-mentioned, then just go ahead and complete the transformation. That is to say, go ahead and shit your pants on the spot and throw yourself on the floor crying.

Snapping and whistling are just rude. This suggests that not only did you not take the time to learn your server's name but you cannot be bothered with the time it takes to say "excuse me." Don't we understand already that if you don't get a side of steak sauce within fifteen seconds then hundreds of innocent children are going to die somewhere in the world? So severe.

Yelling is simply obnoxious. This action single-handedly brings all other people around you into your dining experience and violates both your dignity and that of the staff. Did you really believe that by yelling that you need a fork, a roaming band of protesters would form on the spot and join your plight as support? Nobody cares about your problems, for a couple of reasons: (1) they probably have their own; (2) they already have a fork.

There is never a scenario that makes it acceptable to touch the staff, let alone grab. No matter how pressing and time-sensitive your request is, a violation of personal space takes precedence, and I'll bet the farm that the person you touch will be steering clear of your table for the remainder of your time with us.

My favorite, as an outsider looking in, is the making up of names. No matter how creative these names can be, the caller always comes out looking like a moron. "Chief," "Brother," "Partner," "Captain," "Slick," or "You" are not clever. These are script readings for *Jersey Shore* and should be left in your arsenal for use at the pro wrestling match you're going to later, dressed in your finest Ed Hardy T-shirt. Even worse are names that depict any physical attributes. "Red," "Freckles," "Baldy," "Guy," "Lady," "Server," "Busboy," "Bar-Keep," "Shorty," or any other distinguishing characteristics are out. If you really feel the need to use them, please be prepared for us to turn and respond with "Yes, Halitosis," "Tubby," "Dogface," "Mr. Small Hands," or any other number of names that are going to immediately cast you in an unfavorable, yet truthful, light and probably have the rest of the table staring at your unusually small hands for the remainder of the evening in silent agreement with our assessment. We would love to see you eat a meal while trying to keep your hands under a napkin to prevent judgment from your smirking table guests.

If in the event that you never received a name or just simply can't remember it, there are two things you can do. First is what I am fond of doing myself because I couldn't remember Jesus' name. Observe other employees at the restaurant and wait for one of them to give the appearance that he has a free minute. Get his attention and whisper closely, "I'm sorry to bother you, but could you please tell me the name of our server?" The whisper and close talk imply that you would like to keep this information on the down-low, and unless the employee you picked is a total prick or doesn't speak English (a distinct possibility on both accounts), you should get a whispered response.

The second option is the overall lesson here, as the term "excuse me" becomes very powerful. This term is an attention getter and immediately lets us know to stop and happily attend to your needs. This term should be used every day and everywhere and not just because you belched or expelled gas. "Excuse me" is polite and in just two words shows that no matter how old you are, your parents did a fine job. Watch your volume and tone when using it, but please feel free to flag us down with it. We will stop, even if you're not our table, and we will attend to your needs. Just as when whistled or snapped at, we turn and curse you under our breath all the way to the kitchen, we will praise you and your family openly for being polite to those around us. "Such a nice family at table 20."

Sunday Diners

The anomaly that is the "Sunday diner" came to me in what can only be referred to as an "aha" moment. Not only was the moment captured and instantly understood, but it single-handedly became the driving force behind the blog in which I posted so many of my reflective ramblings. Like a can opener to Pandora's box or the long leather couch at a therapy session, this particular Sunday was filled with observation and set to the glorious sound track of wailing babies, and it was here that I came to a deeper understanding of the world I was living in. It came to me like walking into a freshly cleaned closed sliding glass door. *Smack!*

The typical Sunday diner seems to follow a pattern that should be brought to light, solely to serve as an instruction manual for the layperson, a "what-not-to-do" outlined for those tempted to eat out on Sundays.

I envision the "at home" conversation to play out like this:

"Honey, we got a coupon for a deal at the local watering hole that we have never been to, and we need to take advantage of it soon so we can get busy not going back ever again."

"Sounds good, Hon—*don't* make a reservation for our family of twelve. We will just show up."

And then they come! Manageable droves on spec, hardly constituting a rush and unable physically to fill all available seats in the restaurant, nevertheless, like swarms of locusts they consume every ounce of breathable air and begin dictating the aura of every table on the floor. They arrive and proceed with their "I'm the only person on the planet" mentality like a blanket of thick black smoke from the nearby refinery.

With flip-flops, tank tops, and wailing babies blazing, the demanding begins.

"Hot tea and water for the table... and is bread free? Good, we'll have that... and we have a coupon."

Bless the professional server's heart for abstaining from the tempting eye-roll, instead replacing it with a gracious grin, all the while muttering through clenched teeth, "I'm never going to make rent this month."

Two and a half hours, seventy-five bread baskets, and a bill for $28.50 (after coupon) later, the wildly appropriate (and very well deserved) tip of $1.75 is applied to the bill and the Appalachian family disappears, leaving only the broken crayons and miles of crushed Cheerio crumbs in the carpet (provided of course by thoughtful Aunt Bell and her never depleted pantry from 1942), never to return again... until wait... "Honey, we got a coupon for a deal... blah blah blah."

The scenario is enough to make Clive Barker cringe, but not being a morbid person at heart, I still found extreme comfort in the deeper understanding and strange familiarity of what I was witnessing. I had seen this before, and not just last week or the week before that. I have seen this at every place that I've worked, and not only at my workplaces but anywhere I was lucky enough to visit as a patron on any given Sunday. From Denny's to Chez Fromage the scene is the same and should prove if nothing else that God does have a sense of humor and Sunday in heaven must be his improv night. I can just see God and his angels pushing themselves away from a table littered with the remnants of a fabulous Sunday meal, and while balling up his napkin and tossing it on his empty plate, He mutters something like "Let us adjourn to the theater cloud and watch a bit of the Sunday improv troupe performing in local watering holes across America." (I wonder if this applies to the rest of the globe... remind me to go find out.)

It should be pointed out that not every table in every eatery follows these principles. That is to say, it is by no means a clean sweep of inappropriate behavior, and the average person who goes out to be served on a Sunday instead of cooking a roast for the family at home is not going to be magically transformed into some extension-cord-belt-wearing hayseed who on the other six days of the week is a well-mannered, well to do, straight-backed, elbow-off-the-table diner. However, that does not mean one can't have fun playing the wily bush hunter the next time one goes out on Sunday and quietly observe God's improv performance as an audience member.

Take a look around you and outside the section that you have been seated in, but do pull up short of the neck-bending lean outside your booth, which will get you noticed. While it is true that most Sunday diners are impervious to outside influences and without a care in the world when it comes to what others think about their unrefined ways, there is a brook-drinking fawn in all of us who will spook and run if perceived as being watched.

A good beginner's course would be to go to the obvious lower end of the spectrum to start honing your skills. Go to a diner (like Denny's) around 4:00 or 5:00 P.M. This is the prime "blue-hair" spot that has the older generation coming out to eat "supper" (dinner is lunch, and breakfast is breakfast, and lunch doesn't exist); these wonderful people have been dining for a hundred years in the same booth every Sunday and they know what they like and how they like it. They are the appetizer to the Sunday diner phenomenon.

Then when the time comes, splurge on your own dinner tab and get dessert, even if you usually don't, because around 5:00 to 6:00 the Appalachians will arrive, and you will be able to hear them from the parking lot. You will notice them right away because you have never seen them before in your small town, yet they travel in packs too large to miss. This is usually because the troop consists of cousins, aunts, brothers, and babies, hence the rainbow of age diversity and physical attributes being represented. (*Sidenote: there is usually one man, perhaps the driver of the bus, who looks normal. He has a nice polo shirt tucked into his Dockers and topsiders with no socks. He is not wearing a fanny pack, carrying a camera, or wearing a Bluetooth. This man is "the wallet" and belongs more with us observing the wild pack of hungry dogs, but he has been tossed into this Tim Burton film by marriage. We pause to sigh in empathy for him... aawww.*)

Once you have honed your observation skills at the diner, you are ready to take it to the next level, but let me forewarn you. Like love in high school, you cannot have what you actively seek. All you can do from this point is be keenly aware of the pack when they arrive wherever it may be that you have chosen to eat. If you will them to enter, you will be left unfulfilled and wanting, but you must be prepared to interrupt the gripping conversation you are having over foie gras and a nice Chianti to play the role of the educated one to your dinner partner when the "Sam's Club" members arrive, and simply say, "I'm sorry to interrupt you honey, but you're going to want to see this." Trust me, she will understand.

I have always wanted to start some restaurant political campaign based on the slogan "Friends don't let friends be

Sunday diners!" Not only would we be doing a genuinely great service to those afflicted directly and indirectly by this phenomenon, but the platform itself is unique and chock-full of merit. If nothing else, I would vote for me.

CHAPTER 8

Rounding It Out

Bluer Pastures

Since I began to write this project, I changed venues. I went from beef to fish, and not in the "jumping to warp speed" way that the term implies but rather from steak house to seafood restaurant. My former arena of simple grazing menu items gave way to the vast diversity of seafaring creatures and all the nuances that come as a package deal. Staying true to my game, I will not publish the name the restaurant out of respect for those whom I may inadvertently reference in a less than positive light. We'll just call it the yacht club.

I discovered that there were a few major differences in the land of sea. You will be pleased to know that the finicky diners who provide endless fodder for this project were not only alive and well at my new venue but in fact further armed with the idea of the "questionable validity" of fresh seafood. This notion allows every Tom, Dick, and Harry to peel apart the layers of what should be a wonderful dining experience in the hopes that they may get sick just so they can blame us (a note on food poisoning to come).

My new digs came with a history of thirteen... count them... thirteen years in the game. That's a very long time in restaurant years for single owners to be operating the same watering hole. This was of course a far cry from the four years of struggle and strife I spent trying to put a relatively new restaurant on the local map, as I had just done at the steak house. As I was getting to know my new staff, the following brief conversation took place. Me: "how long have you worked here?" Her: "Oh I'm relatively *new*, I have only been here for two and a half years." *Unheard-of!*

It was my happy discovery in my new home that when guests are shucking and slurping oysters, or cracking and eating lobsters, it becomes impossible to keep white linen tablecloths clean. The solution? Lose 'em. Funny thing about losing tablecloths: ties and coats follow, the volume gets louder and happier, and people tend to have a grander time! Keep it informal and they will associate you with a positively raucous place to be.

The selfish side of this was that I got to shed my once-mandatory suit jacket for a dress shirt with rolled-up sleeves or the seasonal sweater that comes out in the colder months, not only to accompany my shirt and tie ensemble but also to hide properly those unsightly tie stains and shirt wrinkles, as well as the extra holiday pounds that get plastered on the front end during the colder season. I still had the tie, because otherwise people wouldn't know whom to call a dick! But the summer pounds don't come falling off in the form of buckets of head and pit sweat, and I'm cool with that (pun intended).

Tips on Dining Here

A note to all those who make the conscious decision to enjoy the fresh oysters that set the aforementioned seafood eatery apart from the rest, then call later that night to tell us how sick they made you... *not possible!* Food poisoning usually takes more than forty-eight hours to set in, if and when the food product is tainted, which is very seldom. Contrary to popular belief, you are no more likely to get tainted fish than you would be tainted ice cream, so stop giving the little swimmers such a bad rap and do us both a favor... get done puking and Google, Bing, whatever you want, the words *food poisoning* and then see if you can go all Doug and Wendy Whiner on us. Chances are you psyched yourself into hurling based solely on what your three-hundred-pound cubicle mate told you about what happened to him at the all-you-can-eat seafood buffet in the Greyhound bus depot outside of Reno in 1982. We are a far cry from those days and that place.

If you call a manger (me) over to your table and say, "I just don't like it, it tastes a little fishy," I am going to grab the lobster mallet off your table and smash your fingers. There is a good reason your dinner tastes "a little fishy"... it's because it's *fish!* Maybe you should have tried something less fishy... like chicken.

If you feel properly educated now, please put on your Tommy Bahama shirt and linen shorts (we don't care if they are wrinkled) and come see us for the freshest variety of fish that you will ever have, but be aware: you will have a great experience and you will want to come back even if there is a "dick in a tie."

Dearest Cow: I miss you a little and think of you often, but I am very happy in my new life. I wish you nothing but the best in yours!

Getting Full

If one were so inclined, one could pick up this collection of therapy notes and improperly deduce that I am a jaded, opinionated, angry little man who is completely dissatisfied with his station in life and mask my tirades through the more publicly acceptable form of humor, all the while having no respect for the guests and employees who create a place for me to practice my craft. To that I might respond that if I were a betting man (which I am on any given point spread), I would put decent money on your never having completed your degree in psychology—and if you did, you achieved it in the treehouse out back of your friend Clint's mom's house while swigging PBR every other Sunday for a length of time equivalent to the traditional semester. Point being that this would not lend itself to the definition of credible credentials.

The fact of the matter, stated in as little time and in as few words as possible, is that I loved what I was doing, the people I did it for, and those I did it with. I still marveled on most days of the week that I got to go do this thing and get paid to do it. I was constantly reminding my staff when things got a little hairy to step back from the micro side of this industry for a minute, and remember that we got to work in the exact location where people go to have fun. From that standpoint alone, how could we not tolerate the drunken guy at table 4 singing songs from his country of origin? And let us not confuse tolerance with jealousy about the fact is that he has only arrived at the very state we were headed to later, just a couple of hours ahead of our schedule, and it was our task in the meantime to provide him with his due service. Sing on, you crazy German, I will go get you another plate of brats and a stein full of some skunky beer.

On a personal level it may be hard, if not impossible, to envision some of the truths that I feel compelled to share. (*Sidenote: I am not sure exactly why I feel compelled to share personal information other than the fact that we have spent some serious growing time together at this point, and I need to make sure that you can see my smile in relation to the visit. If nothing else, I'm starting to get full; this meal is winding down, and have you ever really had a dessert that tastes like shit?... Exactly... so bring on the palate cleanser.*) For instance, it may be nearly impossible to wrap your mind around the fact that I am a practicing Buddhist who with the highest of respect holds all creatures with a heartbeat blessed and deserving of the benefits due to them all, in the hopes that each of us may pass on our good vibrations to the next person who may be suffering and ease their burden. I truly believe that as a people we are going too fast and need to slow down—and what better place to do that than with a nice meal out? Every two-hour experience in catching one's breath is a tiny step toward tranquility. Hence this very project. We have gone over some rudimentary ideals that will only help you achieve the experience that you are entitled to and shed the go-go-go pace that we have grown so accustomed to.

Further understanding may be achieved if you know that I have ceased wrapping my head around anything destructive either physically or mentally, as I am in long-term remission from mind-altering substances. This path was much easier to find because in my first life (the time that preceded right now) I didn't just dabble in drugs and alcohol, I formed a professional team and played hard every day for years. I am not ashamed to admit that I was good at it—until of course I wasn't. I was so good that I whittled down my choices to three very simple ones: death, prison, or sobriety. Funny thing about drunks—if you want to lead them to a better place and life, then you really have to chop down the final options into digestible bites and then let them take the credit for being able to chew them. Like cutting your child's steak and seeing how excited they get when they say "I can do it!" Yup—that was all you, honey, and daddy's very proud of you.

I have always had the idea of this book bouncing around the empty space located approximately three feet above my ass, much the way a metal ball bearing plunks off the walls of an empty coconut shell, but until I found sobriety, I could never get my fingers to work more than a hundred words at a time. For that reason I am grateful to the person who created blogs and allowed for the electronic journal entries that demand as few words as possible to keeps one's interest, especially because we are on a race track sprinting and don't always have time to read in bulk. This medium suited my sloshy writing style perfectly and provided a much-needed dose of lubricant for the ball bearing rattling around up there.

I have become clear about one thing: we all need to seek out social activities that bring us together. Meet a stranger and let somebody serve you, but respect is reciprocated and smiles are meant for everybody, whether you are on the clock or not. Don't shy away from "paying it forward" and respect life from spiders to aunts (that's clever) and remember that the only way to get anything back in this life is to give something away.

The art of service is not reserved for those in uniform holding a tray of assorted beverages. Service lies within everybody as soon as you open your eyes in the morning and acknowledge that you have been given the gift of another day on this planet and it's time to decide to do the best you can with it.

All of this philosophizing has led to one underlying truth about my life up to this point. In regards to the way this voyage started, I was not "life-stuck" anymore, and I have only the lifeline that restaurants threw me to thank. But wait. There's more!

While one window is gently eased shut, there goes the back door flying open with such velocity that it's a wonder the door didn't come right off the hinges. And while that is a nice analogy, this project of closely examining my surroundings, in an effort to wrap it all up as a gift for you the reader, has led to me once again to a place that I truly thought I had said good-bye to. A crossroads if you will, with more questions than answers. Suddenly, and without recognized provocation, I can feel myself actually coming off the hinges. Uh-oh. *Now* what?

PART II

Check, Please!

CHAPTER 10

The Chasm Grows

Author's Bio

Turn to the back page, flap, or cover of any book written about this industry by any one of the highly qualified individuals who write them, and read the biography you find there. I can guarantee you that 99 percent of these "get to know the author behind the masterpiece" blurbs start with the same opening line. "___ no longer works in the restaurant business," and/or any variation thereof: "___ no longer waits tables," "___ no longer works in the kitchen," "___ no longer manages restaurants," and so on.

It all boils down to the same implied message. "___ no longer cleans his gun with warm tears in the dark just waiting for that one needy jerk to come along and snap his twig." What they don't ever (pause for dramatic affect)—*ever*—tell you is how these people came to find their way out of the cave that the food and beverage industry becomes. Are we all to imagine that because we are sitting here reading their book, they all got lucrative writing deals and are merely farming the mailbox for their royalty checks? That they were forced to leave the business upon completion of their tell-alls because their ten-hour days on the dining room floor weren't conducive to working on the screenplay to accompany their ragingly successful book? I would think not; but again, I don't know.

You see, I myself am in the infancy of this phenomenon. What I can tell you is what happened to me, because whether this little project of mine gets published, circulated, or even seen by another living soul, I will have the same opening line on my biography: "Toby no longer works in the restaurant business." So in turn, Toby is no longer cleaning his gun with warm tears in the dark... you get the idea.

The crazy part is, it makes me happier than an eight-year-old at Christmas getting a shiny new bike. The separation itself took more than a year to sneak up on me, but, I have found a way out of the restaurant game, and I even still possess enough sanity to try to relay my harrowing tale of how it came about.

During that time when I was fully engaged in the odd year of feeling stuck and looking for a door to the outside world while my own started coming off at the hinges, a dear friend told me that most people find their way out of the industry, and/or burn out on it, around the fifteen-year mark. At least, that's how long it took her and the many people she had engaged in conversation on the topic. After dropping this little factoid, she asked me in an unassuming way, "How long have you been in?" (Save for prison reference) I was forced to do some quick math... fifteen years almost to the month. Coincidence or not, I would use her formula as my flashlight to the end of the sewage pipe all the way to freedom. Damned if I didn't find a way of belly-crawling my way through unimaginable filth and muck, in a very Andy Dufresne kind of way, only to come out the other end a free man.

My Own Worst Enemy

I have always held true to the one-line description of myself being my own worst enemy as "I am a jaded individual with a quick wit." To my own interpretation of myself this could be taken as an attribute to "work on" in an effort to make myself a better person or simply thrown aside in acceptance—either you like me or you don't.

The problem—or challenge rather—is not the statement alone. Jaded and quick-witted can be rather innocuous. The real problem is that I listen to my own witty banter and take it for truth. For example, I express my opinion on a grumpy diner that he is probably the type of guy who yells all day at his subordinates and tap-dances the thin ice of heart attack and brain embolism while testing his neck veins' threshold for elasticity, and then goes home and kicks the dog.

This is muttered without thought and merely to get a chuckle out of anybody within earshot at the service station, but internally I am processing this image myself and getting very disturbed by it. I am believing my own lie. Within seconds I have passed judgment on this man and painted him as a physically and mentally abusive person as well as someone who is sprinting toward his grisly and untimely death. I am weakening humanity by one whole person and never for one minute stopping to contemplate the possibility that perhaps his mother is sick and the fact that we undercooked his food and then served it to him cold directly resulted in his temporary anger, the keyword being *temporary*.

I just wanted to make my staff laugh a little, but picked up the sticky mud on my own shoes. Compound this daily for years while I have been exploring my industry through the written word, and all you get left with is muddy footprints everywhere you have walked (suffice it to say that as a restaurant manager, you walk a lot). Sprinkle that with a large dose of Buddhism and higher-power spirituality and you have one very confused aspiring writer, let alone restaurant manager.

At the end of the day I was left with the sound track from every Vietnam movie playing a repeated chorus of "We gotta get out of this place... if it's the last thing we ever do," and while the mortars continued to go off just feet from my face I could feel myself yelling from within and nobody could hear me, "I'm not a soldier anymore... I'm a writer and I want to go home!" Again, but how?

CHAPTER 11

Changes

Before we launch into the logistics of how I get all the way from one day gritting my teeth at the "between shifts" time of the day (2:00 to 5:00 P.M.) waiting for the dinner crowd to start arriving, to the point where all I desire is to have a desk and a window that I can choose to stare out of any time of the day, I really must document some of the tidbits that changed in me personally.

The everything list in me realizes that my served term in Food and Beverage was not entirely wasted and only recently has risen to the level of crisis. Quite the contrary: I had a wonderful time in an industry that attracted my personality type and suited me like a key in a lock. F&B was my answer, and for a great deal of my time on the planet I had been totally devoid of anything resembling an answer. Therefore, I had to realize that some pretty monumental factors had changed in my life before I could do an about-face.

Let us then set the dominoes back up so that we can better start to understand this Rube Goldberg-esque chain reaction that changed the way I feel about the business that had once provided the comfort of a warm towel, but now more closely resembled a kiss from your aunt with the mustache.

Alcoholism

My name is Toby and I am an alcoholic. This is how I introduce myself to a roomful of people on Saturday mornings and some Sundays at the local library, and this is the largest factor personally that lent itself to the decline of my interest in the industry. I am not alone in this.

That last part is important, because for years I thought I was alone—a special case if you will, who got struck by a terrible affliction and decided all on my own to drown any challenge that came down the pike with booze. Long before I actually left the business I was forced to take a pretty detailed look at the things that were making my life difficult to live. So difficult to live and execute on a daily basis that at one point I was convinced that it was all too much for me to handle, and the world would be better off without a drudge like me bringing it down. Relax—I'm writing these words, aren't I, so things didn't go as planned; but at the time it was just one more thing that I managed to screw up. I came to understand that big decisions, like taking your own life, don't manifest themselves overnight. In my own experience, time and unimaginable pain built and accumulated until I just couldn't take it anymore. And the most notable fact during those weeks and months of descent was simply that I never missed a shift at work.

Was it because I needed the distraction of an hourly shift? You betcha. Was it because I was at my absolute saddest when I was alone in my Oakland apartment, so I needed work to provide a distraction? Sure. Did it have anything to do with the fact that I understood that if I could just scrape myself together enough to get to work, I could get behind that bar and start medicating on the company dime? Ding ding ding! Free drinking was the only thing I had to numb the pain, and I had become so good at lying to myself that I began to believe my drunk smirk was really a genuine smile. See, everybody, I'm happy! Really, really happy. So you can all stop worrying now.

All this was really doing was allowing me to sit on the sidelines of my own shitty life for a couple of hours and relax while Mr. Bottle dug the grave a little deeper. Hell, I didn't know. I didn't have an understanding of cause-and-effect reactions. I suppose (in hindsight) I should have been listening a little more attentively in my high school health class when Mr. Jones told us that alcohol is a depressant—that is, it can result in depression. But then again, I should have done a lot of things differently. It wasn't until I watched my dad spiral downward to his own physical demise, based largely on the disease of alcoholism, that it occurred to me that maybe, just maybe, I should take a look at this alcohol consumption thing and the frequency with which it was happening in my life.

The answer at the time was not to stop drinking, though. What, are you nuts? The immediate answer was geographical— in other words, to move home and start not-thinking about drinking because right now it was Oakland that was the real problem. So I picked up my bottle and headed back through the Caldecott Tunnel to my hometown.

I moved home after my failed attempt at gathering answers and took up residence on the corner of the couch that had consoled me before. Turned off the phone and drew the blinds because I needed to go into hiding in the comfort of my boyhood home. I had found comfort here in the past, and I needed the home hug again. But at this point in our family history, things were a little different. Again, I couldn't quite put my finger on the little dark cloud that filled the family room and hovered ominously over my dad in his La-Z-Boy and me on the couch, but with my fingers wrapped around a pint glass of charcoal-filtered vodka and Pepsi and his gripping a similar pint glass full of cheap port wine and ice, we were going to figure it out— or at least pretend that the silent room (save for the clinking of ice cubes) wasn't really filled with the silent internal screams of two men in anguish. *What the fuck is wrong with us? Why are we so unhappy?*

All this time, all this reflection, and all this sadness, and I still never missed a shift at work. I felt better in the fact that I wasn't alone anymore in my Oakland abode. I was home and I was working. What I didn't know was that my dad was more alone than I ever was. I was waiting, seemingly forever, for him to step up and fix things like dads do, but it wasn't happening. I was waiting for him to drop that one sentence that dads say that change the way you look at everything, but nothing was ever said.

I realize now that I was an adult, and that moment in time was calling for me to step up and be a son or support him with something wise from my life's travels that would change the way *he* looked at things. We were two messed-up guys being silently messed up together, each waiting for the other one to speak. I was ten feet away from him on a nightly basis, locked in the struggle of life thinking only about myself, and I couldn't see or stop his own physical deterioration. On March 27, 2009, my dad lost his life to physical maladies caused by long-term alcohol abuse, an event that put a very different spin on the terms "powerful" and "powerless."

Allowing oneself to be removed from the planet in a drawn-out progression by something that you can control is still largely a mystery to me today. Being the glutton for punishment that I am, however, it took four more months of attempts to drown heartbreak for me and my family to figure out my role in this sarcastically semicharmed kind of life.

He was gone, but I was left, so what was I going to do as a representative of the living? I was forced to reflect on his final days. For two weeks I watched a semicoherent dad who was grasping the severity of the situation and, for once in his life, ready to make it different, and I became very afraid of being caught in a moment in time when I was truly ready to change, but it was too late to do so. For the first time in my life, I didn't want to be my dad. I sat across the room from somebody who was just going through that revelation, and it was painful for both of us. I now had my goal.

On August 20, 2009, I walked my shaky legs and darting eyes into a meeting of Alcoholics Anonymous and raised my hand, and life has never been the same since. Let it be known that in almost everything I have ever done in life I seemed to be one step behind the general curve. I am that guy who when the cellular phone world exploded, went around from friend to friend proudly showing everyone my new pager. That being said, getting help with my alcoholism is the only thing to date that I did right on time. Glenn Close in the movie *The Natural* summed it up perfectly for me when she told Roy Hobbs (Robert Redford), "I believe we have two lives. The one we learn with, and the life we live after that."

Send Me an Angel

Who needs a palate cleanser? Not only is it difficult for me to personally relive the harsher moments from my past but to load you on my bus with no brakes and take you for a nice scenic drive in the mountains... well, just who in the hell do I think I am?

A little over a year into my newfound life of sobriety and mental fortitude, and even more active in my role as the best restaurant manager there ever was, I met the love of my life.

Allow me to point out a very poignant fact, that without the restaurant business I would have never worked with one of my favorite employees/friends, Carrie, and without Carrie and her sharp sense of chemistry, I would never have met the woman with whom I planned on spending the rest of my life. Karma, destiny, whatever you want to call it... it all worked out in my favor. Her name is Kristen.

The old saying in AA (and anybody who has even dabbled in that subculture can attest to the overwhelming number of sayings in AA) goes that in your first year of sobriety you should get a plant; and if you can keep it alive, then in the second year get a pet. If by some act of God in the most positive of manners you can seem to hold together enough personal strength to keep the plant and the pet alive for two years, then you can begin to date. I never had a green thumb and I don't really like pets. Plus, this formula was obviously written by somebody in their twenties with a lot of time to experiment, and I'm just not working with that kind of cushion. I have spent far too much time slashing and burning the land for my crops, and then getting too drunk to remember to plant the seeds. My time is now! This little interlude is being written in more of an attempt to entertain than it is intended to enlighten.

Kristen and I did not manifest out of any sense of desperation. We rose from the ashes of an entirely different cliché, namely, "you truly find what you're looking for when you stop looking." I was headlong and very active in my recovery, which translates into I was mayor and sole occupant of Toby Town, and happy to finally be happy. I really didn't need anything else but the understanding of a group of my peers, the love and bonding of my family in the absence of our patriarch, and the accolades from a job that couldn't believe how present I had become in my clear-headedness. Love wasn't even on my radar—hell, I wasn't even looking for sex! I was just happy being peaceful or, in other words, not looking. So we were introduced on a nothing-to-lose platform and hit it off. Carrie was correct in her gut feeling: we meshed.

Within a month we felt as though we had been together for a year. After six months we were living together, and after eight months (of lying to her about personal commitment issues in an effort to build the story, all the while knowing that I planned on making this girl mine) I presented her with a ring that came from my soul. This act of chivalry was merely a reenactment of our next cliché: "you just know when you know."

In my adulthood, I closely followed the restaurant rule that one should never "shit where you eat," meaning that you don't date your coworkers or employees. I say "adulthood" because when I came into the industry in my twenties, it was a different story. My coworkers were the only people I knew or hung out with. Couple that with copious amounts of drugs and alcohol, and of course there were going to be unscripted affairs. The fact that as a manager I never played the role of the creepy, "you want to earn an extra shift?" kind of guy did not detract from the fact that I was single and a healthy, red-blooded American boy. In fact, despite end results, I saw an opportunity in every glass of wine I shared with staff, or every late-night alcohol-laden conversation about past sexual heroics. There was always the remote possibility that the nineteen-year-old I had just hired as a hostess might want to come back to the thirty-four-year-old boss's house and frolic in the predawn hours while we tried not to wake my mom. Who wouldn't want to live that dream? I knew it was a possibility because I had seen the movie before. You know the one: something about an older guy with a German accent and thick mustache who was there to "fix the cable." This is why it's called fantasy, because you'd be more likely to meet Harry Potter playing around in the wardrobe closet looking for Narnia.

Kristen was a whole different kind of fantasy—the type of fantasy that I didn't have to rely on my imagination for, or run right out and buy a copy of P90X to impress. Over regular dessert and coffee at the place of our first date, I quickly laid out my afflictions and dents. I explained my world up front and threw it on the table. There was no doubt that I wanted her, but I didn't want to hurt for her later. I had already grabbed that hot handle, and I wasn't going to burn myself again. So let's just put a sail in this thing and see if it's going to float. I didn't have time or interest in make-believe, so my attitude was, here is my nicely wrapped package of shit for you to look at before you let yourself out, and no hard feelings, I understand. But she threw me a curveball. She stayed. It was as if she took my pile of crap to the garbage, tossed it in haphazardly, turned around with her amazing smile, and said, "Now what?" Real fantasy is so much better than the mental movies. Kristendorph—2 points!

Age

Totally off my radar of items that change was age, but lo and behold, wouldn't you know it, over the course of a fifteen-year stint in F&B, I got fifteen years older. Suffice it to say that advancing fifteen years on the planet results in more than fifteen extra rings inside your trunk, especially when you wait until your mid-thirties to come into adulthood.

I had to admit, and somewhat reluctantly, that I was not merely getting older, I was getting wiser. I was growing up. One of the facts that can be laden with an odd balance of sadness and excitement is that when you grow up, your old toys don't look the same. Ask any box of Woody and Buzz Lightyear toys and they'll tell you the same thing. Restaurants became the box and my staff and the people who came to see us became my Mr. and Mrs. Potato Heads. Even as I write this, the analogies are flooding my mental imagery. This is nature at its finest, but I found that no matter how many times you have seen the *Toy Story* movies, you can't quite be prepared when it happens to you.

This phenomenon ripped me right back through the wormhole to the last time I was being forced to "grow up" without my consent, and before I knew it I was in the powder-blue rocker-recliner in the bedroom I occupied in high school, writing terrible poetry about love and wondering if this confusion and awkwardness would ever end. The year had changed, but the script was still the same.

If the truth does reveal itself in the form of lessons learned, then no matter what the year may be, I should have found more comfort in knowing that the spin cycle of life would end and once again I would be wiser and no worse for wear at the end of it. But if nothing else, haven't we all learned that I seem to be a glutton for punishment? And all of this was happening at a time when I was at my most cynical and pessimistic, so of course my illness, in attitude terms, wasn't the head cold it appeared to be, but a rampant case of cancer... one I would not survive. The only difference between now and the days of pimples and gangly limbs was that I was in a position to take out a lot of people with me in a burst of misguided leadership. Thank goodness I chose to document the experience as opposed to going all fully automatic on a staff that required my leadership or the self-righteous diners who visited me on a nightly basis.

Just what was this new diet that my age was requiring for life, and how was I to shop for and feed it? The conclusion that I came up with, moments after removing myself from the boxed restaurant and the toys it contained, was that it was high time that I be paid and tested based on the merits of my intelligence rather than my tolerance for pain. I realized that for many years I had been collecting a paycheck based largely on my threshold for pain. Nobody was coming out of the back room and asking me to solve equations, or creatively put into words the operational directions for a specific piece of machinery; they were instead coming at me nightly with their mind-boggling problems of undercooked food, reasons for missing a shift, or asking me to work sixteen-hour days in uncomfortable shoes.

My career had become more of a "take this, take that" or "left, right, uppercut, body blow, body blow" type of existence, but my age in the beginning allowed for the punishment (even welcomed it). Now in the dawning of my maturity, I was realizing how sore I had become and just how nice it felt to lie down on the mat as opposed to getting up. I needed a nap. I needed to begin using the eight pounds of flesh that sat on my shoulders as opposed to the rest of the body that absorbed the blows, but I couldn't find the cushion of comfort between paychecks to look for the Promised Land. Between working nights and writing about how confused I was, there was little time to play online poker, let alone shift life gears. This growing-up thing was not growing on me and never had. Up to this point I had lived very successfully running from maturity (yeah, right).

I found myself right back to the lonely bedroom of the 1990s, wanting only to be eight years old again, with problems no more pressing than should I play army guys with Jeff or *Star Wars* with Joe. If only my problems didn't involve money, things would be better.

Then it dawned on me: I have been flat broke a couple of times in my life, but never hungry. I have paid for a pack of cigarettes with pennies but still smoked them in a room with a door and a roof. I have been completely alone in the world all by myself, but always had somebody to talk to about it. The bottom line became simple, as it often does, and that was to just let go. Trust that I would be fine, and not unlike the love I found with Kristen when I truly wasn't looking, the opportunity to leave the business arose when I knew that I would be fine, come hell or "high waiter."

CHAPTER 12

Parasitical Annoyances

What started out as a tongue-in-cheek potpourri of hilarity has ended up getting under my skin, and I mean really under my skin. This was not my desired goal.

In reflecting on the early stages of writing this book, I would be forced to admit that my only motivation was to give myself an avenue for blowing off some steam. With that release valve as the foundation, an evolution began to take shape; like a ball of Flubber, this work started to take on a life of its own. The imagery of gremlins being fed in the bath after midnight comes to mind—or to those a little less specific-minded, I seemed to have a tiger by the tail.

Something happened that set this transformation in motion. Upon reflection I would have to imagine that the catalyst was the "Sunday diners" phenomenon. This was what first piqued my interest and brought together the two worlds of F&B and writing. The phenomenon was too good and far too entertaining not to share with the masses. But how and where should this forum take place?

As I've mentioned before, when I was introduced to the world of blogs (long after the initial hype had died down), I truly thought I had found the key to the universe. Not unlike most technology (remember the pager), I was late to the party on this one, but wanted credit for planning it. So here I was being the first person to discover online journalism, and eager to use the vehicle. I opened and designed the blog "Careful, This Could Get Messy" with one rule only: I would share everything that I was privy to seeing and experiencing behind the scenes of whatever restaurant I was working in at the time, but I would never mention any actual names of people or places. I was aware that what I had to say was certainly not going to make everybody happy, and being as this was the Internet, which led my imagination to picture millions of people being exposed to my semantic blockage laden with humor within weeks of my blog's launch, I certainly did not want to run the risk of any slander lawsuits that would halt the process. So one rule set in stone and I was on my way.

On a weekly basis I poured my observations and attitudes onto the keyboard and, with little to no thought, hit "submit" before returning to the trenches to find more fodder for the blog. As many transitions happened in my life, I became fanatical about it—even more so as I was getting positive feedback.

A Frankenstein-esque reanimation began to take shape. I began to seek conflict or hidden nuances that required my attention so that I could put a semihumorous twist on them and throw them to the tech-savvy followers of my blog like so much meat to the lions. Apparently there was more going on in the restaurant business than I was aware of, and "Sunday diners" served as a gateway drug to the mounds of crack I uncovered, Not unlike the "good times" brought on by the early days of crack, I was soon cold, pale, and shivering, offering to do unmentionable things for the messed-up restaurant experience. In short—the blog was beginning to breathe on its own and learn to say phrases like "Feed me, Seymour."

The idea of the blog led to the grander idea of a book. But this book couldn't just be a collection of short gut-blowers, it had to be more. More than two years into my exploration of the blogosphere, the idea became larger. My gremlin morphed into a desire to use all of my anonymous tales to teach you the readers how to work at and dine in restaurants with a higher rate of success based on what not to do. This plan rode completely on the idea that nobody wanted to be "that guy" once "that guy" was pointed out—and I was going to do a lot of pointing.

As I continued the hunt for the douche in the crowd, I began to be a more successful hunter. Point being, it was a douche I sought and it was a douche I found. But handling this once-elusive specimen in captivity slowly began to lead an innate dislike for these people. What a vicious cycle this became. I needed to get as close to the douches as possible to learn and document the very douchy things they did so that I could launch my project, but the closer I got and the more time I spent with them, the more uncomfortable I became. The whole project was still steeped in humor and presented on a platform of entertainment, but some serious crossroads were beginning to be constructed. And despite what products were being presented, inside me it was not funny. I was getting jaded. I was becoming a monster, and these douches had become parasites who were truly getting under my skin.

Here are some examples of the things that were happening all around me that were leading to my pervasive feelings of disdain. Where once I was able to simply disregard such daily happenings and do nothing more than perhaps train the staff how to deal properly with them as they arose, I was now carrying them with me to a fault and could not let them go. The following is a collection of the specific behaviors that served as the nails in my coffin. Take a bow, people, you beat me at my own game.

Don't Be a Celiacshole

In the ever-evolving world of F&B, a (relatively) new and worthy adversary has emerged with a vengeance. Over the span of what seemed like just months, but had really been evolving for years, there arose celiac disease.

To those unaware, this is an autoimmune disease of the small bowel that occurs in genetically predisposed people of all ages, often starting in middle infancy. However, for those aware of this predisposition but not directly affected by it, one could deduce that one of the most common symptoms is that it can turn you into an asshole. (Ironic.)

Allow me please to take a sympathetic step back while celiacs catch their breath and decide whether to keep reading. I have nothing but the utmost sympathy for anybody affected by any disease, and this is simply a rant against the small percentage of those who treated me (and others in the profession) like the very people who gave them their illness. It seems to me that this illness can be directly compared to kids and the ADHD epidemic, which seemed to gain momentum and popularity as soon as Ritalin was invented and hyper kids could be muted. Bottom line is that yes, many people are affected directly by an intolerance to gluten and must eat accordingly; but just because you get a lower belly pain when you eat three loaves of bread in one sitting or get a little farty when you pour a gallon of soy sauce over your sushi does not mean that you get to jump on (or drive) the bandwagon. More to the point, it's not our fault that you did these things.

So when you begin your meal by taking on a tone of royalty telling me about your allergy and I, in turn, tell you exactly what items on the menu are safe for your consumption (because I was that prepared of a manager, and so was my staff), don't wave me off dismissively as if I were the royal food tester and then stare aghast at my incompetence when I bring you your very safe soup of the day with a fried plantain chip in it, because you thought it was a corn tortilla chip.

Generally people who can't even carry out the simple task of providing a dining experience based on your dietary restrictions don't get to take responsibility for the daily operation of an establishment, and just in case you're keeping score, I had the keys to the place.

Here it is—celiacs have had a tough run of things while the general restaurant industry has struggled to adapt menus and education policies for staff to familiarize themselves with this new allergy. In addition, I can totally dig that for the past five years you have remained in your house eating nothing but chicken broth through a strainer behind drawn shades while the rest of us have tried to catch up, but the bottom line is communication.

All guests have to do is make a phone call before their time at a restaurant, preferably at the time they make their much-desired reservation, and ask if the establishment is equipped to handle a gluten-free dining experience; most are. Then remove your empty Kleenex boxes from your feet, pull your hair back into a ponytail, and lose the tattered bathrobe, then step into the light and come enjoy a fine meal devoid of anything that may cause you pain. But leave the attitude back at the house with your collected bottles of urine because I really don't want to be tempted to crumble a cracker into your salad dressing... but so help me God! Naw, I'm just playing... could you imagine?

Hall of Douchery

Let us now embark on the people who are to the dining experience as Sugar Ray was to boxing in the sense that they seem to stick and move, stick and move, and you never see them coming. I mean, you know you're boxing cause you're in the ring, but you're never quite prepared for what may happen. Endurance and realization practices must be honed to a fine point as these professional pains in the ass drop their jaw-busters as effortlessly as we flush the toilet. You may not even realize you got douched until you get back to the safety of the service station or kitchen, when all of a sudden it hits you! If nothing else, these types deserve literary acknowledgment for making service so much more colorful than a desk job.

In mid-experience with these special people you feel the visceral urge to react physically to them. It has been my experience that you want to either laugh, punch, or scream at them. In an effort to portray the tone of my internal monologue while these experiences were happening to me, I provide a key or legend at the end of each entry as follows: *DR* ("desired reaction") = *laugh, punch, scream* (or any variation of the three).

"And a Diet Coke"

This is one of my favorite regular occurrences. Three-hundred-plus-pound woman comes in for lunch. After she has successfully *not* been seated at a booth because the table position is fixed and allows no room for her Buddha belly, she launches into her order like she woke up thinking about it. "I'll take a burger, rare, with extra cheese. Side of mayonnaise, no lettuce but extra relish. I'll have onion rings *and* fries, please, with cheese and chili, no salad, and to drink... a Diet Coke."

What? Save for the argument that diet soda has a different flavor profile—I'm aware of that—nonetheless, any person's first introduction to diet anything was not based on the desire to have a different taste. It is clear that merely uttering the word *diet* makes this woman feel better despite the fact that her burger dream last night is coming true because she'll be damned if it puts one foot in the grave... she is prepared to prevent that and any weight gain that might ensue with a Diet Coke. *DR: laugh/punch*

"Oh, no she di-ent!"

Again, true story. I was working at the fine-dining steak house at the time and we opened our doors for service at 5:00 every evening. When we unlocked our doors one Friday night, this woman poured herself in like she hadn't eaten in months and had been waiting in her Chevy Lumina for us to open. I couldn't find out whether she was expecting anybody else or dining alone because she was on her phone. So I just sat her at an available table set for two in the vastly empty dining room.

Turns out she wouldn't need the other seat because, unknown to me at the time, the person she was dining with that evening was on the phone and was going to stay there. This lady not only stayed on her phone the whole time she was in the restaurant, but she was loud to boot. "Oh, no he di-ent!" and "Girl, you crazy!" or my favorite, "You bet-cho ass!"

I suppose all of this would have been fine if this annoying diner had eaten her kids-meal entrée only and then left before our first reservation at 6:00, but no. This lady had a four-course meal, with cocktails and wine, that lasted a little over three hours.

At the time I could have sworn it was a test by the corporate office to see how management handles challenges. One of the best twists of the evening was how absolutely annoyed she was whenever her server had to ask her any questions. She would roll her eyes, yell "Hold up!" into the phone, and then address the server with "What?"

"I am so sorry to disturb you, but I left my mind-reading pants at home. I just need to know what you would like to order."

You can only imagine how badly she wanted to rip my heart out when I was forced to ask her to keep her voice down because of complaints from other diners. She paid the bill, applied an 8 percent tip, and walked out with a handful of complimentary mints, all while laughing at whatever her BFF was on the other end of the line saying to her—"That was so-o-o funny." I swear you can't make this shit up. *DR: punch/scream*

Asks Then Tells

The bar top is where you get most of your tales of douchery, for two reasons. One is the consumption of alcohol, and the other is that your server (the bartender) is tethered to the very place where you are consuming your libations and unable to leave; therefore, that long-suffering individual is always available to be brought into any mind-numbing conversations that may be taking place.

Of all of the "you gotta hear this" storytelling, or cancer-curing conversations that take place over any given bar top, my favorite is still the people who are trying to figure out some random but very important piece of trivia or fact that they just can't reach an agreement on. Here comes the invitation to the bartender to intervene with his or her vast knowledge of all times and events. The conversation goes like this:

"Hey, youse. What restaurant was here before this one?"

"It was the Chowder House."

"Naw, no, you're wrong—it was something else."

Okay, listen, fucker—a few things really quick. First, it *was* the Chowder House, and I know because I work here and I know the history of the building enough to talk about it to the customers. I also know because I am sober and you are drunk enough to not know your kids' names. Third—don't ask me a question and then argue with the answer. If I don't know the answer right off the bat, then I'll tell you, "I don't know." I have nothing to lose by you thinking I'm not smart. Lastly and most important, get the fuck out of my bar and go down the street to the place that used to be Sam's Hofbrau and ask them what it used to be, but when they tell you it was a hofbrau, keep your mouth shut! *DR: scream*

"Smells like fish"

Let us start by setting the scene. It is yet another bustling night at the seafood establishment that pays my bills, say around 7:30 P.M. Enter the four-top who are approximately ten minutes late for their reservation, but that's okay because they have a reservation and I have been holding their very desirable table eagerly awaiting their arrival. They push their way to the podium and give us the name while one of the two females in the group says rather loudly, "Let's not eat here, it smells like fish."

At this point any one of the other people in the party should have turned around, rolled their eyes, and said equally loud, "Shut the hell up." But no, they actually turn and leave without a word. Well, we certainly found out the hierarchy in that group of douches. I felt a little bad for them not staying, as they must have meant to make a dinner reservation at the candle shop across the street that smelled less like fish than a seafood restaurant. What exactly did they want the Bay Area's Best Seafood to smell like? Would it have been better if our restaurant smelled like funnel cakes and corn dogs? *DR: punch, then punch again*

"We should be compensated"

It is a blustery and miserably wet night. So much rain in fact that the water in the gutters in front of the restaurant threatened to rise all the way to the door. I wouldn't have blamed anybody for deciding to ditch their reservation, yet there were still some who had probably been looking forward to this all week, and bless their souls a very few who had still showed up to enjoy the warmth of candlelight and a professionally cooked meal.

Enter crusty old lady. Before even rattling off the name on the reservation, she demands as she shakes the water from her blue perm, "We should be compensated for coming out in this weather!"

It was a cute ice breaker. I agree with her through a chuckle and ask for her name to check against the reservation. That's about when she lets me know she's serious. "Really. What are you going to buy us for coming in tonight?"

Holy shit! She's for real. While I appreciate her being there, she has to see that of all nights we are in no position to be giving anything away free. We should actually be hiking our prices to make up for the people who decided to stay home. We were already not going to make our numbers, but now Ms. Retirement Community feels entitled to more than she is willing to pay for. You want compensation? Here's a voucher for a thirty-minute water aerobics class at the community pool; but don't go asking for an extra thirty minutes for free when you jump in and get a little wet. *DR: laugh/punch/scream*

"Can I get you anything to drink?"

I would love to open this tale of douchery with saying that lunch shift is the worst, but it's not, so I can't. Truth is, breakfast is the worst, and if you have ever had the good fortune of working a breakfast shift at a hotel, then kudos to you and the personal fortitude you must possess. I can say that lunch is the worst if your restaurant doesn't serve breakfast. So let's say that... where I worked, lunch was the worst.

This douche didn't make it any easier. He swaggers in not looking like he belongs anywhere, let alone a decent eatery. It is clearly a business lunch because the guy with him had on a suit and was approximately twenty years older than his guest—who had Johnny Depp pirate hair, never took off his sunglasses, and brought his own thirty-two-ounce 7/11 Big Gulp. He sits down, moves his water glass to the side, and sets his store-bought beverage at the head of his setting. I can overlook the appearance thing of this under-the-bridge dweller, but unless this guy found you at 7/11 and you were on foot, find somewhere else to ditch your really big beverage. I imagine this guy on his way out of his office and saying, "Oh, hold on, I forgot something," then going back and getting his thirty-two-ounce Mountain Dew. "Okay, I'm ready, let's go." *DR: laugh/punch*

OpenTable

I was fortunate enough to be working in the business when the OpenTable software came on the scene for the first time, and was still in the industry as the footsoldiers began to learn how to manipulate the system. For those unaware, OpenTable currently has a monopoly on the electronic reservation system and floor-management software that is crucial for the success of any restaurant. At the time that I am writing this, you can believe that if there is a computer monitor at the front podium of your favorite restaurant, it is running OpenTable, and anybody who has worked in the business speaks its language.

Enter annoying patron stage left. This is a general rant that encompasses the multitude of people who crane their neck for a glimpse of the screen and any information that confirms that yes, indeed, they did have a seven o'clock reservation on a Saturday night. These people are usually made up of past or current restaurant workers who have used the system before, or family members of somebody who waited tables through college only to later explain at the Thanksgiving table how OpenTable works as a way to break up the awkward silences.

They know who they are, and here's what they do. First off they have probably seen one too many romantic comedies in which the Steve Carells or Matthew Brodericks of the world cleverly steal somebody else's reservation and make it seem so campy and innocent. Let me tell you now that in the real world outside Tinseltown, stealing somebody's reservation is not cute... it's stealing, and if you are ever discovered even attempting this feat you should be punched in the neck.

So they come in at the busiest time of night when the eighteen-year-old hostess is already frazzled and inform her that the party of seven for Johnson, reservation at 7:45, has arrived, and they are ready to be seated. The hostess tries mightily to find the reservation and raps at the keyboard but never takes her eyes off the screen and the information that it is spewing forth.

What is happening simultaneously is that "Mr. Johnson" knows he's about to be exposed as not ever having made a reservation and the other six hungry people in his party are going to know that he's the douche who lied to them and the hostess. This is precisely the time that "Mr. Johnson" thinks he can "help" the hostess my moving to her side of the podium or by craning his neck around the screen or, on some occasions, physically stepping behind the podium and standing inappropriately close to the staff. He then begins pointing at the information on the screen, perhaps the area that should have displayed his name if he had followed procedure like a responsible adult but didn't, and he begins to explain that he knows what he's looking at 'cause he's no dummy.

"Right here! Right here! My reservation should be listed right here! The girl told me 7:45!" Never mind the fact that he can't provide the name of the girl he spoke to because all he knows is that it's a pretty good chance that a female would have answered the phone if he *had* called.

Listen up, "Mr. Johnson," we know you're lying. We knew you were lying as soon as you opened your mouth. If you weren't, you wouldn't be so manic. Only arm flailers and scene makers have something to hide. The point is that we already established you're a liar because you're not in the system, but now we are trying to figure out how to accommodate you anyway, and your actions are making it that much easier to admit defeat and let you know, "We sure are sorry for the mix-up, but we couldn't possibly get you in any earlier than 10:30." *DR: scream/punch*

"We're ready to order"

This last one is another generalization that should serve to help anybody who knows they are guilty of this subtle infraction with detrimental results. If you really can't admit to yourself that you have committed this dining snafu, then heed the warning and be aware that if you, or anybody else you may be dining with, get the urge to wander down this ill-advised path, hear my voice calling you a jerk, imagine the volumes of staffers around the "water cooler" calling you the same thing, and back out of it as fast as you can.

As mentioned previously, the good servers are the ones who are constantly mapping out next moves, and doing so usually four to five steps in advance. Not only are they moving gracefully across the floor with a purpose, but they trick you into thinking you're the only table they are waiting on that night. Allow me to paint a picture of the internal monologue of a busy servers mind: "Iced tea for table 12 with extra lemon, table 23 is ready for their check, side of mayo for 15, and the little girl at 32 dropped her binky under the table." Now a quick map is mentally drawn to facilitate in the most efficient route: "Stop at 32 to pick up binky on way to service station to print up check for 23. Print check, pour iced tea, and get lemon on tray while telling your busboy to drop mayo on 15 seat 3. Drop tea, turn around and drop check and stop, smile, and thank them for coming and hope they have a great Sunday."

Then you, the patron, chime in. "Miss, were ready to order." Sure, you're on table 6, not even in her section, and nowhere near the server's mental "to-do" list, but you're ready to order. So she'll just knock this out really quick and give the order to her coserver at the service station when she's done. Won't be more than five minutes out of her valuable time.

"What can I get for you?"

This is where you proceed to ask the difference between grass-fed and free-range, if the fish is sustainable, how long have we been open, any gluten-free menu items, and any number of other questions that suggest that you are most certainly *not* ready to order. Let the record show that if you are going to raise your voice above table conversation in the hope of getting heard that you are indeed "ready to order," you'd best believe that when the server gets to your table, everybody in your party will know exactly what they want and in which order they are going to say it. You were in such a hurry two seconds ago, but now want to ask how my childhood was. The reality is that all you wanted in the first place was attention, and you probably wanted everyone at the table to know what a real go-getter you are. "See, I can summon the waitress with one bellow." But to us as well as to your guests, you really look like a king douche. We know what we are doing, so please try to return the favor. One of my favorite things to say in that spot is, "Let me know when you're *really* ready," and then walk away. It dramatically affected my tip at the end but served as therapy on the fly. Worth every penny. *DR: punch, scream, punch, punch*

When all of the aforementioned instances happened, either as isolated incidents or the ever-present generalization, they all served as shovels to the grave that I was slowly digging for my career. The fact should still be pointed out that the very douches who commit these crimes against service staff are most certainly the minority of the daily happenings in and around the watering hole. More often than not, the patron is of polite, appreciative, and pleasant demeanor—in other words, hardly worthy of literary immortalization and not worth the time or the ink spent trying to bore the tears out of anybody I have been fortunate enough to keep hostage in the name of entertainment.

The best part about douches is that 99 percent of the time, they are totally unaware of what a huge douche they are being and will read any description of themselves believing beyond a doubt that it is about some other douche. It is almost as if being a huge douche has become second nature simply because you've committed the act so frequently. I purposely left the other 1 person to represent the person who is aware of the wrongs they execute and most likely act that way on purpose as a big act of defiance. Perhaps something may have gone terribly wrong for them in another part of their life causing them to be permanently jaded—so much so that they have unknowingly made the decision to stop trying to fix the shit in their life and go ahead and trudge through it while tracking it all over the carpets of those of us lucky enough to keep company with them.

The Greek tragedy aspect of the whole venture is that I used to just laugh and document; but now, being so helplessly locked into my drive to make the industry more positive, I am seriously thinking that perhaps this one percent were merely restaurant managers once upon a time. Highly probable.

The Cricket in the Bedroom

They say that hindsight is 20/20, and the longer I live, the longer all of those cute grandparent sayings come to fruition. Here I am in the "salad days" of my new professional life, sitting on the proverbial porch and looking back through the haze while still trying to decipher what led me to this point. I'm not in a bad place at all—quite the contrary—but the analyst in me can't seem to leave well enough alone or believe that yesterday is gone but today is a gift (hence the word *present*) so I should stop looking back.

In retrospect, there were many specific moments that led me to leave food and beverage service. Though they got somewhat lost in the weeds of day-to-day operations, the following incidents should have served as more of a warning than they did at the time. They should have been a bucket of cold water thrown across my face while the bells were ringing and the gates were dropping, because at any moment a five-hundred-ton train was bearing down on me to take me out of the food game. Instead I bent down to pick a flower.

Christmas for the Staff

Every Christmas is a good time at the restaurant for a few reasons. First and foremost is that people are out in droves to spend more than their allotted disposable income on presents and spoils. As I mentioned earlier, this directly equates to big sales in retail and restaurants. So servers, bartenders, bussers, hosts, runners, and owners are getting fatter from the calendar days from Thanksgiving through New Year's Day every year.

Let us now explore the missing components from the list of the fat getting fatter. Notice that two key players are not represented on that list: the kitchen staff and management. We get to work ten times harder than any other time of year for exactly the same pay. That's not even the problem, though. As a matter of fact, most of the people I have worked with who hold these illustrious positions (myself included) enjoy the holidays immensely for the pace and tone that they bring into the workplace. People are (generally) jovial and in a celebratory mood, and there are a lot more of them. Have you ever been to a packed bar that was depressing? Not even at a funeral will you find that oxymoron. So, yeah, coming to work was always a little easier when you were submerged in holiday cheer, and it has been scientifically proven that smiles are contagious. (Okay, I just lied so that somebody would believe that factoid and have a better day because of it.)

In addition to the general vibe of any operational dining room floor, there is the underlying fact that management gets bonuses at Christmastime. I mean, c'mon. Is the ownership really supposed to turn a blind eye to the fact that they are making a lot more money and their managers are not? In addition, they are forced one time every year to tell me "Good job" and "Thanks for keeping our heads above water" so that I will return and do it again for another eleven months and twenty-nine days. Anticipating the bonus is nice.

So here is how it went for me on my last year in the business as far as Christmas bonuses go (remember—indicators of a spoiling career). I actually helped get the bonuses for the staff ready that year in an effort to help the boss. Forty-five employees all got gift cards to the very restaurant where we worked.

But wait! Before you assume that this is my launchpad into tirade, allow me to talk you down and explain why this is actually a cool gift. We had an operational fish mart on premises, and every day we could buy and take home the freshest fish within a seventy-five-mile radius. The gift cards given to the staff were as good as cash as well as for after-shift drinks (no limit), so if you were so inclined, you could get plowed after work one night or get one polite after-shift drink every night for quite a while. Lastly, the gift cards were based on seniority, which is great! If you had worked in the kitchen for ten years (which most guys had), you got the largest amount, and the greenhorns in the kitchen knew your clout based on your gift card size.

I couldn't help but begin anticipating what I might get this Christmas, based largely on the fact that I was one of only two managers and the higher-ranking one at that. Certainly it would be a cash gift, probably a few hundred dollars. It wouldn't be a gift card because we already had in-house expense accounts, so that would be redundant. Plus, in my past jobs, management bonuses always came in the form of money, because that's what we made for the owners all year, so that's what they gave back. It's kind of the circle of life.

The day came when I went into the office that we all shared, and one of the two owners turned in his seat and ceremonially began with the opening line, "We would like to thank you for all of the hard work that you have done this year." Here it comes, man, a day/week/year changer. He turned around to retrieve my parcel from under his desk and handed me—a bottle of wine.

You have got to be kidding me, right? I immediately began looking for Ashton Kutcher and tried to stifle my laughter, but before I could go all postal he followed it up with the same kind of envelope that I had been stuffing for the staff for two weeks, addressed to me. "Okay," I thought, "here is the cash prize and maybe it is a gift card, but that's cool cause it will be for a lot more than I saw others getting because I'm his manager." Considering it impolite to open such bounty in front of others, I took my sealed card to the nearest dark corner like a squirrel with the last acorn before a winter freeze. I opened the card, and inside he had written the same exact line he opened with: "We would like to thank you for all the hard work you have done this year, Merry Christmas." That was it, a bottle of wine and a clichéd message on a card.

Did I mention that I am a recovering alcoholic? Not only that, but I am not ashamed of my recovery, so my staff knew the facts, if for no other reason than to not push the after-shift drinking too heavily on me and respect my situation in life. Have I ever sat down and talked about it with the owners? No, but really. You know my mother's name, you are friends with me on Facebook, subscribe to my blog, and follow me on Twitter, then turn around and give me a bottle of wine for my Christmas bonus? The foundation began to do more than crumble; it was weakened beyond all hopes of repair.

New Yorker Cartoon

It wasn't long after the bonus debacle that I began unofficially to look for alternatives. I figured I could make my profession last for as long as I needed to, but my heart was cold and black toward the specific place I was working.

Naturally, I started down the path that any other extroverted person would follow. I began to talk out loud about my growing disdain for the place. Never did I speak to my staff, and not usually at the restaurant during shift, but solely to my friends and family. I needed advice because I was in dangerous waters, the current was picking up, and I have always been ill-equipped with the mental tools to handle the tides when they get choppy.

One night, though, the two axes converged, bringing together both support group and professional arena. A friend had dinner at the restaurant. I explained in hushed tones my growing angst and my ideological fantasy of scrapping it all and pursuing writing. Without hesitation he told me that he needed a tech writer at his budding bioengineering start-up. The rest, as they say, is history.

I began to moonlight between shifts. Working in a positive environment with palpable excitement among some of the smartest people I have ever rubbed elbows with during the day, then it was off to the restaurant trenches at night. Like so many other instances in my life to this point, I needed to get both hands firmly wrapped around that scalding-hot pan handle searing off layers of flesh, just to make sure it was warm.

The female contingency of the ownership duo at the restaurant I was mentally separating from loved to clip the cartoons from the *New Yorker* and leave them on the desk of the male boss to laugh at. It was endearing and nonthreatening to me and something for us all to enjoy behind the scenes, nothing more, nothing less. However, the arrival of one of those cartoons ended up causing one of those "nail-in-the-coffin" days, the day that I decided that two jobs was far too many for me to have.

I have never been one to welcome or embrace conflict of any sort. I really do hate to let people down, so giving my one-month notice (industry standard for managers) filled me with nerves and anxiety. As disenchanted as I was about my career choice, I was certain that the owners were none the wiser. Did I mention that they gave me, a recovering alcoholic, a bottle of wine for Christmas?

I walked into the restaurant with my heart racing, knowing that it was all about to end, but questioning whether I was doing the right thing. I made a quick stop in the service station to check the nightly specials and take one deep, centering breath before I headed up to the office to face the music. On the servers' bulletin board was a cartoon from the *New Yorker*. Strange, because her cartoons had never made it downstairs to be shared with the staff before, and it hadn't been there yesterday, but there it was for all of the staff to see. The picture was of a man sitting at a table in a restaurant, clearly intoxicated, and yelling at the passing waitress, *"It's not alcoholism if the wine scores higher than 90 points!"*

Did they hate me? Did they want me to leave? What was going on with their recurring-themed jabs? If nothing else, I wasn't nervous anymore. I was driven on piss and vinegar. I marched upstairs and told them that I would be leaving the restaurant for other ventures in exactly thirty days. They seemed genuinely shocked, then angry, then sad. All of the appropriate behaviors in all the right places, but not for a couple who had never made me feel welcome. I did it to them, but I didn't care! *Hasta la vista*, restaurant!

Internal Debates

Long before the "nail-in-the-coffin" experiences began to make my mind up for me, but shortly after the seed of "what's next" was planted, I went through a series of hindsight moments without really knowing I was going through them at the time.

One particular realization was of the prolonged variety, meaning that for quite some time the notion had been percolating in the back of my mind without being directly faced. Though I didn't know it at the time, this phenomenon is one of the biggest red flags of a career in demise. I will lovingly refer to it as the "grass is always greener" syndrome.

I had been in F&B for so long that I naturally forgot I even remotely possessed other marketable skills. When the two paths of uncertainty cross, as mine so dramatically did, some very bizarre and unforeseen conclusions are drawn. Because I was so unhappy in my current situation I began to imagine what the future could hold. None of the perfect-world stuff where broccoli tastes like ice cream, just questions like, what could I do to pull myself up by the bootstraps while at least maintaining a similar salary? (Don't mess with my money, man!)

This is exactly where the other path came in and eased me into the false belief that I didn't really possess any other skills remotely close to the talent and years I had in the restaurant game, so any future plans would still have to be centered on the industry. This is very similar to what is referred to in alcoholic recovery as a geographic—that is, moving to a different place because your life sucks in the mistaken belief that your damaging life patterns will change with the scenery. Until you address the real issues, there will be no reprieve from your problems. This meant that what I needed to do was begin exploring options outside the restaurant business—options that didn't include working weekends, holidays, and nights, or options that tested me more for talent and intellect rather than flexibility of spirit.

Let me remind you that this preceded the "wine bonus," the New Yorker cartoon, and the employment offer from my friend. I may not have realized it at the time, but I was in the first stages of the leaves turning brown and all of the compromises that come with it. That being said, I quickly decided that for me to be truly happy, I should go back to waiting tables. I would cut my workable hours in half and still maintain a decent income, and I could use the extra time to write. (*Sidenote: this kind of logic has led me into hot water more than once. It's the logic that immediately leaps to all kinds of rosy conclusions and leads to ideas like "I think I'll just wake up tomorrow and win the lottery." Never really works out like you plan.*)

I immediately began to conduct small and private conversations based on confidentiality with my staff, starting with questions like "If you don't mind my asking, how much do you make in a week?" I had a pretty good idea about the various levels of income based on the schedule I crafted, specific strengths and weakness of the staff, and the tax documents I was overseeing in regards to declared tips, but I wanted a clear-cut idea of what I could expect to bring home based on my talents. I knew I was a good (nay, *great*) server, but it had been a hundred years since I had relied on that talent for my income.

The response I got from most of them to my "if you don't mind" opening was the same. My staff immediately drew their own conclusions, and they were right. They knew exactly why I was asking, and they shared with me how many other managers they knew who had chosen the same path.

This irked me. I didn't want to be like everybody else, but I was also able to immediately fast-forward to a few years in the future and see that I was still going to be struggling with feeling as stuck as I was that very minute a few wasted years down the road. As butt-hurt as I was about getting called out on my covert operations, I came to feel very grateful that my peers unknowingly led me away from becoming a server again and changed the angle of my approach. Of course, things would get worse before they got better, but isn't that an indicator of something worth fighting for?

Taking Notice

Right about this time of turmoil, I began to look at everyday occurrences in a far different light. I suppose that if I had been examining all along the time that was passing, the way I am doing now, I would have had to admit that while observing my surroundings, my eyes began to open. Sounds crazy and obvious, but the mind has a funny way of coping with routine that one finds unacceptable but is unable to change. Apparently I was able to go great distances across time and space being constantly slapped by indicators, like a lifeguard on a beach slapping a partially drowned man, and only now was I able to focus enough to hear my Hasselhoffian hero yelling "Breathe, damn you! Breathe!"

This is precisely when I began to notice the inordinate number of past managers coming in to eat in the restaurants they had previously left behind for greener pastures—a variant on the ex-F&B employees' biographies that begin with "So-and-so no longer works in the restaurant business." Not only were these people coming in to eat, but they were doing so at prime times in the week, usually solo, and staying for a long period of time.

The eye-opening aspect of this phenomenon was revealed to me by the most unlikely of sources. My comanager had asked me to cover his Saturday shift weeks in advance because he had something important to attend to. No big deal, this happens all the time; but because there were only two of us as managers on staff, his request resulted in a long day for me. It simply meant that I would be working his opening shift and then bleeding it right into my closing shift—a sixteen-hour day that netted no extra money for me (God bless the salaried employee). However, it did give me credit for a favor in the future. In the restaurant business, you just kind of jump in and swim. You never allow yourself to be consumed with the hours or the work. I knew that would be the case for me. I would just come in at 10:00 A.M. and work, and because I wouldn't be seeing my comanager, my brain would be tricked into believing that I was supposed to be there all along. Then before you knew it, midnight would roll around and I would be going home.

But not on this day, I'm afraid. At 9:00 P.M., the busy time for the bar, my comanager came in for drinks with his friend. (Just in case you are keeping a notepad next to you and feverishly scribbling protocols about "how-to," please note that this is an absolute no-no. Get your shift covered, and then disappear. Don't come into the only place on the planet that you should be if you weren't out being an ass with your shift covered.) Then, in an attempt to be hilarious in front of his buddy, he added insult to injury; he started ordering his drinks from me with a raised voice, as if to say, "Be snappy about it." The only thing that kept me from digging his drunken heart out of his chest with a dull spoon was that he was the only person on staff who wasn't aware of what an ass he was for even being there. That is to say, behind his back the servers were independently approaching me with the same "that's fucked up" sentiment. It helped.

After that night I began to notice that the managers who had worked there long before my time came in with such frequency that I not only knew who they were, I knew what they were doing now, how they ran the business when they were king, and what they liked to drink. This began to sit very uncomfortably with me. There was no reason that I should even know what these people looked like, short of my own mental images from remember-when stories being thrown around the break room. Yet here they were, filling the staff with stories of what their normal lives were like and how they had never been happier. They were like recently paroled prisoners going back to visit their cellmates in their new shiny suits. It was not cool.

But again, through pain we learn lessons, and I began to see that these despicably happy people were not gloating about the new restaurant they worked in. They were talking about how they switched careers successfully. So like a good scientist I shut up and observed. I comped them their drinks and took information as payment. More than anything else, I took their example and allowed myself to dream the impossible dream that it was possible somehow to set sail from this world in search of something better and actually reach land. At this point it was a matter of mere moments before I invested in my own *Niña, Pinta,* and *Santa Maria.*

Dream a Little Dream

As soon as any situation finds its way into the subconscious, one should take a gigantic step back and take a good long look at that situation, for better or worse. In the wee hours of the night and in the furthest reaches of my dreams, that is what was happening to me.

In the service industry, things happen all the time that lead to people's expectations not being met. Most people call me over to the table, prompting the ever-popular and very generic opening line, "What seems to be the problem?" But for some the simple floor manager is just not enough, and they feel it is their duty to inform the higher-ups of any travesties that have transpired. This practice is even more rampant when you take into consideration that any successful establishment in a small town is made up of approximately 85 percent regular customers who have been patronizing said restaurant for more than fifteen years. At this point they don't bitch about their table not being ready because they are pissed, they do it out of a self-inflated sense of duty. They truly believe that the owners rely on their reconnaissance missions to construct their successful business.

Here's how it goes. Something happens during their meal that turns them off. Probably it's no more than a slight variation on the remarkable time they had the previous week, but to them it is wholly unacceptable. They don't ask for me because they have seen six of me come and go over the years, so what do I know? So rather than squeeze fake sympathy and a free order of calamari out of me, they bite their tongue until they get home. Three glasses of wine later they have the courage that could stop a robbery in progress, and they sit down to their computer to write an e-mail directly to the owners.

I came in on a Saturday to find that a Friday patron (let's call her Ann) had written the owner (let's call her Karen) about her embarrassing evening. She had spoken very highly of us to her cubicle mate for years and was finally getting an opportunity to bring her into dinner. (*Sidenote: we are already set up to fail before the night has begun because these office manatees have been putting us on an unattainable pedestal for years.*) So she begins to tell Karen how the soup came out cold, the drinks weren't strong enough, they didn't get their favorite table, and they felt rushed.

These are all very small gripes that could have been handled by me the night before to everybody's satisfaction, but no, it's now a written complaint. At this point Ann not only names her server (let's call her Maggie), but single-handedly blames the whole thing on her and finishes her rant with the threat that *if* she ever comes back the restaurant again she'd better not have Maggie as a server or she will leave.

Karen is now forced to respond with a written e-mail laden with apologies, complete with the offer of a free glass of wine the next time she is in, completely dripping with verbal honey and signed *Yours truly, Karen.* This is called "taking the high road," and it's always done this way, regardless of how she or you really feel.

Well, not in my dreams it's not. (*Sidenote: one of my most least-favorite things in life is any person who starts a sentence with "Oh my God, I had this dream last night..." You should be able right there to tell them to get fucked and walk away. For the record, I'm not doing that, so pay attention.*) In my dream I walked into the office like any other regular day and was confronted by this very e-mail. All normal so far, until she brought up that because I was the floor manager and I didn't handle it that night, I was going to be responsible for the apology e-mail. I was to sit and write it immediately and bcc the owners so they would know what I offered her for free the next time she came in. Then they left me alone to construct my master apology.

Dear Ann:

Let me start by offering my most sincere I don't give a shit to you and your guests. Your soup was served to you cold in the hopes that you would get pissed and leave, saving your thighs from any more embarrassing cottage cheese or varicose veins; but in typical fashion, you couldn't take a hint and stayed for three more courses. May God have mercy on your stretch pants.

As for the drinks not being strong enough, I am sorry. Sorry that we don't all drink a handle of charcoal-filtered vodka before 3:00 P.M. every day, making every store-bought drink seem weak in comparison. Why don't you explain to me how we can expect to make any money by pouring drinks to your standard of toxicity?

I understand that you didn't get the table you usually get, but you have to understand that the table in question is near the front of the restaurant and bar. Did you happen to take a look at that thing you brought in as your guest? I'm assuming her last name was Merrick and she had an affinity for elephants. Between her mouth full of crooked Chiclets and your cankles there was no way we were going to let anybody directly look at you.

In regards to your server, Maggie is the best server we have on staff and is always happy to be here and wait on trash like you because tips like the ones you left her last night might put her and her two kids out on the street, and she only rushed you because she assumed that you were late for an AA meeting.

In closing, don't come back, we don't have enough food and our chairs are too old to take the load.

Yours truly, Karen the Owner

I woke up with an enormous sense of satisfaction—not because I finally got a chance to say exactly how I felt when faced with a disgruntled guest, but because I remembered to bcc the owners so that she could see I signed her name at the bottom.

This was yet one more indicator that perhaps it was time to go.

CHAPTER 14

Opposites that Used to Attract

At this point of my separation from the food and beverage industry, I was knee-deep in my reflective phase. Not having made any physical strides per se toward improving my situation, I had resorted to picking it apart while I was still playing in it. Truth be told, I was carving out more and more time for the analytical portion of my day just to stoke the fires of interest enough to show up at all. Did I ever mention that in the fifteen years I was immersed in F&B, I only logged two sick days? And those were because I was truly sick. So I'll be damned if I was going to let a little thing like a cloudy emotional state brought on by the relentless torment of my choice of profession get in the way of my work ethic.

So here was the revelation that I stumbled across one day when silently playing on the swing set in my head. The very factors that had wooed me into this business so long ago were now acting as the biggest deterrents to staying in it. This was a remarkable discovery because we are not talking about a few items here. We are talking about the whole kit and caboodle.

The discovery had a domino effect. I realized, for instance, that I just wasn't attracted to the binge drinking aspect that I'd formerly held as dear as my own child, and from there I began tracing other nuances to see if they still held any attraction. Well, what about that... nope, can't stand it. And this... nope, don't want any part. Well, surely I still love this part... nah, holds no interest for me. Holy cow! My former attractions had become deterrents all across the board. Was I growing up, or changing, or both? Is this what grown-ups act like, and does this mean I'm going to start listening to AM radio in the car because the programming is really "easy on the ears"?

These are very odd questions to ask oneself, especially when you're only thirty-seven years old. Here then is the list of items that once drew me in but were now spitting me out fifteen years later.

Drinking

Anybody who has been paying the slightest bit of attention could have seen this coming. I'm pretty sure I would have been an alcoholic without the F&B industry, but it certainly didn't help. I am fond of the saying that if you go to the barbershop long enough, you're going to get a haircut.

I loved the culture that was bred on the dining room floor and then later behind the scenes. A culture that was centered on drinking—serving it, selling it, talking about it, hiding it, working through it, doing it every night and every day. At the time I began serving tables I truly felt that I had found my tribe, consisting of an eclectic group of people who drank just like I did, fast and hard. We were pushed hard to learn as much as we could about what we were selling and serving, so calling all-night benders "cram sessions" was seen as both funny and practical. If you tell any lie long enough you are going to start believing it, and so I did. I began to believe that this is the way the world operates, and all of the nine-to-fivers who were stuck in their cubicles were doing it wrong unless they had a secret bottle stashed in a drawer.

Every person who has ever bartended is familiar with the expression "one for you—one for me." Drinking with patrons are a surefire way of ensuring you get a good tip. I learned awesome tricks for hangovers, and the sun lost its touch for telling me the appropriate time to drink. Another expression that many foodies are familiar with is "it's five o'clock somewhere," and it was... so you see, it's all under control. Until it's not.

Shortly after I got sober, people would marvel at how I could stay in a business that was so focused on drinking, and I would explain that it was different for me because I was in charge of the booze behind the bar now. I was a manger, so I couldn't just run around drinking on the job behind the coatrack. All that was fluff and feather, because the four months between my father's death and my sobriety date were laden with benders. I was using my manager card to order drinks under assumed table numbers, and then comping them off the imaginary tab. I was bringing my own bottle of rotgut wine into a restaurant with seventy-five thousand dollars in wine inventory and drinking it in a soda glass. I knew the tricks, and they began to weigh on me until I stopped.

My new cocktail was sobriety with a splash of professional angst, and that made me hate other drunks. People who came into my bar and were loud and slurry dug at the very core of me. I was resentful toward my staff who brought two cases of Coronas in every Friday and Saturday night to drink after their shift and left me waiting while they finished so I could lock up. I grew very tired of our wine-tasting classes preshift every Saturday night, when the staff got to try some new arrival to sell tableside that night, and every Saturday without fail I was handed a taste that made me sweat with temptation. I was beginning to see that it was not normal for people on the clock to be handed alcohol by their boss—at least it shouldn't be—and I realized I no longer loved that part of the life the way I used to.

Free Food

How can anybody find anything negative to say about free food? Not even I, as inured to the business as I had become, could turn the draw of free food into a deterrent, right? Quite the contrary. Remember that I was becoming older and wiser, and one of the biggest tradeoffs for wisdom and age is that one's body becomes far less resilient to the ravages of a poor diet.

For anybody who has never worked in the restaurant business, allow me to squelch the fantasy that as employees we all walk around tasting marvelous morsels of food in eager anticipation of the meal being prepared for us by a professional chef right at eight o'clock every night. That couldn't be any further from the truth. We are subjected to the very food that people come in to eat all the time. The smells and sight and sounds of sizzling plates and sauces are right under our noses the whole time we are working, but one of the quickest ways to get a business shut down is to catch a person picking off a plate. In every place I have ever worked, there was an unwritten code of moral ethics about this, and you never breached it for fear of being strung up by your peers. True, I never did any time in a Chili's or TGIFridays kitchen, so I can't really attest whether the movie *Waiting...* is accurate, but I never worked with anybody who would put their fingers deep into somebody's plate of pasta before it got to the table.

Don't get me wrong: I have witnessed dishwashers eating out of the trash and a barback finishing somebody's cocktail, but mostly we just looked at those types like they were sad and probably in some capacity needed it more than we did. As a manager, I was forever stopping servers from stealing bread from the roll warmers, but that was just to make sure they didn't have food in their mouth when they served the table. Calculations don't always go right when computing chewing time versus timely service.

In most of the places where I worked we did get fed as a part of our shift, and at the others we were offered incredible discounts on food. When the food is provided by the establishment it is called "family meal." And why not? That is exactly what it was. Served after shift was over and the last guest had left the building, pans of food were (usually) hastily thrown together and put out for a "slop-the-hogs" smorgasbord buffet for degenerates. The last of the rice with some fish that was going to get thrown out because today was the last day we could sell it. A green salad with almost expired toppings and a potpourri of bottom-of-the-something squeeze bottles for dressing. My favorite would be when we had something left over for a banquet and would be forced to eat it until it was gone. Once a party had ordered cold cuts as an appetizer for two hundred people and not one person ate any of the salami, so guess what we ate for two weeks as a staff? We had salami everything—salami sandwiches, salami potatoes, salami pasta, and, my favorite of the week, salami and mushroom risotto. I cannot even begin to tell you what bad "bed partners" salami and risotto make. And there were two factors that were never taken into consideration with family meal that put my love of free food six feet under and pushing up daises: time of consumption and healthfulness.

Days Off

When my career in F&B was in its infancy, you will recall, I worked at a private golf course. In California (could be in other places around the country, too, but I have never worked elsewhere, so I really couldn't tell you) private golf courses are closed on Mondays in order for the greens crew to restore the course back to preweekend glory, since of course, most of the rounds are played on Saturday and Sunday. To the cogs in the machine (i.e., the staff) that meant that we all collectively got

Mondays off. We also got to golf the course on those days, working around the added challenges of moving mowers, sprinklers going off at random times and places, aerated greens, and greens without any flags marking the holes.

Most foodies will tell you that their days off are in the middle of the week, regardless of where you work, for the very obvious reason that whenever regular folks are out spending their money, we are working to take it. In the beginning, this was a dream for me, for a couple of different reasons. One was that nobody except foodies had days off in the middle of the week. The fact that we were dramatically outnumbered as far as workforce by the multitude of cubicle rats our schedules gave us free rein over the world of consumerism at odd times.

We never waited in lines at the movies, restaurants, or anywhere for that matter. There weren't enough people out to constitute a line even if we all collectively went to the same place at the same time. We never had to sit in the front row at the movies, unless we wanted to because we were stoned out of our minds and had already seen *Finding Nemo* twice and thought the perspective change would be "trippy" (true story). Most bars and restaurants host what they refer to as "industry night" in the middle of the week so as not to impose on their regular paying customers while tipping their hat in respect to those who belonged to our supposed club. We never drove around looking for parking. In the busiest of cities, we were again one of the few, and we pretty much had carte blanche out in the world.

This was awesome in the first few years, largely because my social circles were made up of other foodies, and so, save for the few who couldn't get out of their pajamas, we were a roving band of misfits helping to stimulate the economy in an otherwise barren world between nine and five Monday through Friday. As management jobs led to my severing connections with people who were now my subordinates and boundaries began to be redrawn to encompass some of the cubicle rats who were once so despised, the off hours became less and less attractive.

Accelerate the timeline of life a few more years and throw in a "regular" worker-bee girlfriend, and the schedule once regarded so highly became downright unbearable. I even successfully lied to myself for the first few months of our relationship that one of the reasons I knew we were going to last is that our schedules were opposite, so we never spent any time together. How could a person ever tire of another when they barely got to see each other? It was like a yearlong honeymoon. It turns out that this excuse was just one more line serving to justify my annoying career long enough for me to buy my own bullshit—and I wasn't buying it anymore.

The scheduling woes really clipped me on the chin in January 2010. My brother and his two little ones make the holiday trek back to California from Iowa every January, and we do Christmas part two for my nephew and niece. It is a great time, complete with stockings, pajamas, gifts, anticipation, Santa Claus, and family. The adults snap pictures and drink Champagne and nonalcoholic beer all day in their slippers while the house is all abuzz with the sounds of new electronic toys and pull-string dolls with the smells of a baking ham permeating the very clothes we are wearing. One would never know it was just a Saturday in mid-January until Uncle Toby had to excuse himself to go put on his jacket and tie because he had a ten-hour Saturday shift to work. "You all have fun, and I will see you next year."

That was my final straw. I realized at that moment that I had been missing out on a lot of important things in life because I had to go to work, and that did not sit well with me. All at once facts and figures crowded my head of all the wedding invitations I said no to because I was too busy working some wedding for a customer. I even missed funerals because they are planned when most people can attend them. I was no longer a member of the wolfpack howling at the moon in the middle of the week, I was a loner tired of making friends with tumbleweeds and saying no to the people who sought my company.

Just like that, in January I muttered under my breath, "These hours suck," and my viewpoint would be forever skewed until I got myself some "regular" hours.

Regular Exercise

The job called for constant physical endurance, and because of that I didn't sit down for fifteen years. It was not uncommon to see pedometers attached to the hip of some foodies who were interested in learning the exact number of miles they walked in a day. In the country club where I worked, stairs and vast open rooms were part of my everyday trek. My comanager and I used pedometers for a month one winter and mathematically figured that we walked an average of twelve miles a day. On an average work-week of five days a week, that averages 3,312 miles walked in a year.

That is the same as if I walked from California to New York and then back to Bloomington, Illinois, but let us please be real. The restaurant game is where averages go to die. For instance, for a weeklong event in the summer I worked all seven days, twelve to fifteen, hours a day, getting ready for our flagship tournament. Traveling between the pro shop and the men's locker room brought me into contact with three flights of stairs, two vast dining rooms, a bar, a foyer, and a courtyard. This distance, traveled no less than three times an hour, consisted of nearly a mile of territory. In short, I was logging at least double the average twelve miles for seven days straight. Just to give the same sort of visual example, the mile really walked would be like walking from California to heaven, through Limbo (after meeting God), and back to the summit of Mount Everest.

In the beginning I loved it. I ate terribly rich foods at ungodly hours, drank a bottle of wine and a six-pack a night, never sniffed the inside of a gym, and was in the best shape of my life without ever having to think about it. Now fast-forward to my final stint in the seafood restaurant, where the floor space was one-eighth that of the country club and flat, save for the executive offices being up a flight of stairs.

This wasn't initially a problem because while a manager is at work, there is no need to be upstairs-until the end of the night, that is, when the servers need to get paid out on their shift. I hardly need to mention that the staff always needs to get paid right when I'm ready to sit down for the first time of the night, or that it wasn't uncommon to find me enjoying my first cigarette in six hours, only to have a server ask me to get something upstairs right that minute. Or the fact that they seemed to take great pleasure in waiting until I had come down the stairs, having just completed one task, before asking me to complete another upstairs task before my foot was off the last step. In this tumultuous time, it was not uncommon for me to rip the head verbally off the asshole server who started any sentence with "Oh, were you just up there?"

Point being, I was still over my daily dose of low-impact cardio. Even after spending $170 on my Dansko shoes that were custom-fitted for my arches, my feet were a wreck. Fifteen years of punishment had led to bunions and blisters, and every stairwell was met with a deep sigh of submission.

Nothing was worse than the time I bought my first pair of Dr. Martens. I was so excited and naive that I threw away my old pair of work shoes the minute I got the Docs and put them into full-time service immediately, only to find out three days later that proper protocol is to bring two pairs of shoes to work and wearing your Docs only two to three hours a day until they are broken in. I had crispy shoes on my angry feet for ten hours a day, six days a week. I could hardly walk, let alone carry a tray gracefully, and seriously cried on the third day from frustration and pain.

I was over this whole exercise as part of the job description thing. When I landed my desk job right after service I quickly gained ten pounds of muffin top, and it was the most glorious muffin top in the history of man.

Never the Same Day Twice

One of the factors that distinguishes youth from maturity is the desire to mix things up in order to maximize learning potential by keeping things interesting. Foodies in general have a shorter-than-most attention span and they tend to possess the maturity level of the average twelve-year-old; this is one of the reasons they have many of the tools required for success in the restaurant game. Places deep within themselves are awakened, and many find themselves succeeding where once they had been misfits at almost everything they'd done before. There is a deep divide between those of us who toyed with and or executed making the restaurant business a career and those who got out when it was still just a job.

Early on we career F&B workers became very aware that school was a bust, though not for the reasons one might think. For most of us, it was just boring. For myself I can truly declare that if it weren't for drama class and the smoking section in the parking lot, I might never have gone to school merely to protect my 1.7 GPA. So we would find ourselves in the wild world of F&B, where the hammer is already down on the pace accelerator, and no matter what happens during one particular shift you can rest assured that the very next day will hold a completely different hand of cards. This phenomenon feeds our very souls and is what makes us able to hold on for just one more shift, and in turn hold on, day after day, for years. No wonder we eventually all make model citizens in Alcoholics Anonymous: we have been living one day at a time for our whole lives.

Funny thing about maturity, though, is that it seems to happen with or without your presigned approval. I don't want to go so far as to brag about how I matured, or walk around with my nose turned up and an air of "you just don't understand" toward those just entering the business, but I will admit that, not unlike the other categories in this section, something changed in me, and I was seeing the object of my employment from a different angle and in a different light.

I was tired of looking at my clock before I went to bed and envisioning what time I needed to wake up the next day based on what time my shift was. I didn't have to set the alarm, mind you, because if you have to set your alarm to wake you up anytime after noon, then you have bigger fish to fry. But I did have to visualize what my day was going to entail because I never really had a handle on it. For instance, on Wednesdays I had my manager meeting so I went in an hour earlier; on Mondays I opened the restaurant and submitted payroll but we did a good job of cleaning on Sunday night so I could go in hour later than usual; on the second Friday and every Saturday we had wine training and I hadn't written the test yet so I'd better go in early on Thursday; and this Sunday my hostess would be at her boyfriend's karate tournament so I needed to go in early to check messages, do the floor plan, and hopefully get somebody to cover the front, but just this one Sunday. Next Sunday would be my usual schedule. This is the daily and weekly punishment that I endured. And these were the only occurrences that I was made aware of through advance notice.

This scenario speaks nothing of the ever-popular call in sick by the hungover employee, the depleted bathroom supplies or sodas requiring a run to the store, the twenty minutes it was going to take if the printer acted up, the reconfiguration of the banquet room because half of the forty people expected are delayed in Chicago, or the last-minute phone call from the owner letting me know that he is going to be passing the restaurant in twenty minutes on his way home from the cabin and wants a to-go order for seven people brought out to his car.

I found myself asking anybody in my general vicinity of my voice what they did that day at their desk job, and the responses were generally the same. "Not much." This struck me as such a beautiful response in its simplicity. I began to realize that the top of the mountain for me was to be able to say "A little of this, a little of that" to describe my day whenever anybody asked. Not the "Do you have an hour, and I'll tell you".

Somewhere along the way I found my shadow, grew ear hair, started listening to AM radio, and any other number of I-got-older signs that seem to pop up to fill in the "You're becoming like your parents" checklist. I didn't ask for it to happen, but by the same token I wasn't upset that it did. I wanted to know what my month looked like in advance, and then decide whether I felt like sharing that with people when they asked. You want to know what I did this month? "Not much."

Wine Pairing

Your honor, I would like to submit into evidence that in no way shape or form does the defendant's previously discussed alcoholism play a role in the following testimony (not really). Now that the air is clear and I can proceed without feeling the judgmental sneers of all the regular drinkers (or "normies" as they are referred to by us drunks), let me tell you that for me, wine was the biggest draw to my profession and the single ingredient in any success that I happened to carve out in all my time in the trenches. It was the garlic to my spaghetti sauce—all but the final seven to eight months, that is.

The country club where I worked was smack dab in the middle of a vineyard. Miles and miles of grapes owned by Wente Vineyards in the Livermore-Pleasanton area totally surrounded the Tuscan-influenced mirage that I called home. Learning wine was not an option, it was a prerequisite, so thank goodness it held a natural fascination for me. I came into the country club scene, as well as into my newly chosen profession, with absolutely no knowledge of wine beyond that somehow it came from a grape squashed by barefoot people stamping in a tub at some Belgian summer festival.

I distinctly remember being at an old girlfriend's family Christmas and being asked by her unassuming mother to explain the dark green bottle of Chardonnay that she received from an out-of-state uncle. Not being one to shy away from any opportunity to appear to be an authority on anything, I polished off my pontificating boots and launched into my blind sermon with "Well, it's a red wine." Sometimes in the deep postsleep thoughts that invade a person's psyche while greeting the day in the ritualistic morning shower, I find myself remembering that moment and allow myself to mask my tears in the downpour of nozzle water. Have you ever had one of those strong sensations that you would like to kick your own ass? That's what I go through every six weeks or so.

One particular day when I was still a fresh and very wide-eyed server in the land of fine food, my executive chef summoned me to his kitchen for a very important task. I was to gather the staff to meet in the private dining room for a tasting of the roasted duck confit he had created for that night's special, and then run to the cellar to retrieve the 1996 Concannon Petite Syrah. Somewhere in the ensuing twenty minutes of time I was lost forever, never to return the same human being. I left a wine boy, and returned... a wine man!

That was when I first truly experienced the sensation of pairing the correct wine with the correct food, the head change that comes from the melding of two entirely different ingredients, and the lightheaded feeling of actually getting "drunk on food." Before that moment, I realized, I had only ever eaten for survival and never for pleasure. I wanted to hike the nearest mountain and yell at the world about my discovery and then chastise all initiates into this mystery for keeping the secret from me for so long. Even today, enjoying the proper wine with food is something I miss about what my disease has dictated I can't do.

But enough of this exaltation, let us not forget that currently I am a jaded little man who cannot find any value in any aspect of F&B, not even wine. In my former years, I asked to take every dinner party being hosted by my bosses because I could talk about wine to the table all night, and even if I was wrong I sounded right. I could sell you a sponge of vinegar by telling you it was this year's trend. I kept the bar manager hostage in our bar for hours after we closed, going over the wine list, trying different samples, and comparing wine-tasting notes. I put away my golf clubs on Mondays and headed out into the Livermore Valley, which I had only been looking at for so long but was now going to drink, and not in the bowling-alley shots of tequila way, but rather the aficionado way. I worked private dinners at people's homes that were catered and paired by our club and described in intricate detail to the guests what we would be drinking with each course and why it was chosen for that specific food. I was becoming an expert in my field, because as stated earlier, my head had been peeled back by something I just had to understand.

My passion on this subject remained untarnished for years, until one day I realized that 90 percent of the people I was talking to didn't give a shit about what I was saying. From the people dining in the restaurant to my staffers who were hired to convey the very message I was trying to relay with just a fraction of the passion I felt on the subject, I might as well have been talking about brussels sprout juice. (*Sidenote: I love brussels sprouts. At this point it's the people I hate.*) I suppose one can only go so long talking and not being heard before somewhere a mechanical rod breaks, and instead of suggesting a nice light Paso Robles Pinot Noir with the macadamia-encrusted halibut you suggest the milk... 2 percent for that extra fatty flavor. So then came the affliction that I had ignored long enough, and I was forced to make drastic changes to my consumption practices. Spoiler alert! If you have ever wondered if you can receive help with alcoholism and merely cut back on your drinking, the answer is *no*. It's kind of an all-or-nothing deal and not the "sake with sushi only" type of choice. So now did I not only desperately want to stop talking to people while their interest ebbed and flowed, but I wasn't even allowed to have an educated opinion on the flavor. Screw this industry and the grapevines it swung in on, that '70s Vietnam movie ballad is starting to play in my head again.

So there it all was laid out before me, like a cricket in your bedroom at night. Hear me out on this. Have you ever had a cricket get into your bedroom before? It is single-handedly the most annoying occurrence on earth. First of all, the cricket is certainly loud enough to keep you awake at night because a cricket's leg endurance is seemingly endless. Second, they are smart little buggers (pun intended). As soon as the light goes on, they stop. As soon as you creep within five feet of the tiny headaches in the dark, they stop. This is exactly what my end was like. I was getting increasingly irritated and impatient, but as soon as I turned on the proverbial light to take a look at any solutions, there were no solutions or problems to be found. Just like the cricket scenario, it took randomly smashing general areas out of frustration until the proper alignment of stars presented the solution.

Then, what seemed to be instantaneously, I was out. I was hired in a different profession, with a completely different structure, and with a completely different group of professionals. I felt like the minor-league ball player who gets a call to go up to the big leagues. I quickly packed and boarded the bus and really never even said good-bye to my old team, if for no other reason than I was toting this shit-eating permagrin that I didn't want to rub in their faces.

When I got into the management side of the restaurant game, I realized that if I was going to make a run at this thing as a career, I had to have goals. My goals were simple. Continue to succeed as a floor manager until being given an opportunity to be an assistant general manager, after which I would log a few more years learning and grinding until I became a general manager. Then I would be happy. Then I would be making the big bucks. Then I would have validation.

With my goals met and the title of GM firmly in place, I finally realized that I was just as life-stuck as I had been so long ago when I was sitting on my friend's porch wondering what I was going to do with my life. The only thing that had changed was time and a few details. A little bigger in the belly, a lot less hair, and more aches and pains than I had in my youth. So with all the strength I could muster, I once again packed my hobo's handkerchief with whatever marketable skills I possessed and headed into the great wide open, but this time I had sobriety, the love of a good woman, and a hell of an idea for a book.

About the Author

Tobin (Toby) Tullis no longer works in the restaurant business (I DID IT!) Since then, he has traveled the world delivering affordable healthcare, written operation manuals, writes the monthly restaurant review column for Alive Magazine and hungers for more avenues to create.

Born and raised in the small Bay Area town of Danville, California, he took the leap of faith not so long ago and moved 15 feet north to the small town of Alamo. There he resides with his lovely wife Kristen, their son Braden and daugther Harper.

With the knowledge of different worlds and the comfort of small town living, Toby set out to document his accidental 15 year experiment in human behavior while dining in or working at restaurants in this his first book.

Want help with your own restaurant? Toby offers training and motivational seminars, restaurant evaluations, and strategic planning on how to bring more success to your business. Let the lessons he has learned assist you in maximizing your investment. Use the contact page on *www.writtenbytobin.com* to inquire.

ABOOKS

ALIVE Book Publishing and ALIVE Publishing Group
are imprints of Advanced Publishing LLC,
3200 A Danville Blvd., Suite 204, Alamo, California 94507

Telephone: 925.837.7303 Fax: 925.837.6951
www.alivebookpublishing.com

CPSIA information can be obtain
Printed in the USA
LVOW13s2230140514

385867LV00004B/228/P

3 1901 05393 2242